NEGOTIATE, INFLUENCE, PERSUADE

MICHAEL YARDNEY

NEGOTIATE, INFLUENCE, PERSUADE

HOW TO PERSUADE OTHERS TO DO WHAT YOU'D LIKE THEM TO DO

Published by Wilkinson Publishing Pty Ltd
ACN 006 042 173
Level 6, 174 Collins Street, Melbourne,
VIC 3000, Australia
Ph: +61 3 9654 5446
enquiries@wilkinsonpublishing.com.au
www.wilkinsonpublishing.com.au

ISBN: 9781922810120

A catalogue record for this book is available from the National Library of Australia

Design by Tango Media.

Printed and bound in Australia by Griffin Press.

Follow Wilkinson Publishing on social media.

WilkinsonPublishing

wilkinsonpublishinghouse

WPBooks

Note to reader

This publication contains the opinions and ideas of the author and is of the nature of general comment only and does not represent professional advice. It is not intended to provide specific guidance for particular circumstances and it should not be relied on as the basis to take action, or not take action on any matter which it covers.

This book has been written without taking into account the objectives, financial situation or needs of any specific person who may read this book, which means that before acting on the information in this book, the reader should seek appropriate professional advice.

To the maximum extent permitted by the law, the author and publisher disclaim all responsibility and liability to any person, arising directly or indirectly from any person taking action or not taking action based on any information contained in this publication.

ACKNOWLEDGEMENTS

■ ■ ■

In early 2006 I approached publisher Michael Wilkinson with the manuscript for my first book.

He was initially courteous and polite, but not overly enthusiastic — until he read the manuscript. Then his gutfeel gave a new, and then unknown, author (me) a chance.

Since then Michael Wilkinson has published my eight books but for years he's been encouraging me to write a book on negotiation, as he's seen my negotiation skills in action many times over the years as I've grown the Metropole Group of Companies nationally to the point that we've recently been awarded the accolade of Australia's leading property consultancy in 2019 and 2020.

Achieving this was far from a solo effort. Similarly, this book would not have been possible without the support and encouragement of certain people who have contributed to my life in many ways.

In particular, my wife Pam for encouraging me, supporting me in every way and putting up with all my late nights and weekends on the computer. She endures my almost fanatical attitude to business and property and continually encourages me through the good times and through all the things I still need to learn. I am humbled by her love and devotion, which I try hard but never quite succeed to match.

Special thanks go to my family, including our children and grandchildren for their love and encouragement.

Further thanks to my business partners, Ken Raiss, Mark Creedon, Brett Warren, Kate Forbes and Greg Hankinson and the whole team of property professionals at Metropole. And thanks also to our many clients whose collective inspiration has given me strength.

Important thanks go to Johanna Leggett whose editing and writing skills have taken my ideas and concepts and turned them into flowing dialogue.

Over the years I have read almost every book about wealth creation, property and negotiations ever written. I have learned a lot along the way and there are many ideas sprinkled throughout this book that I have learned from others. I guess I had to learn everything from someone at one stage, so I am sorry I cannot acknowledge everyone — I really can't remember where I first came across many of my strategies.

Where I recollect first hearing about an idea I try to give credit where it is due, but if I have omitted mentioning your name, please excuse me as I shamelessly acknowledge borrowing other people's good ideas picked up from observation or from conversation, books, CDs, DVDs, podcasts and seminars. As knowledge about negotiation, influence and persuasion isn't one individual's sole domain and there are really no secrets, I can only assume that these people also learned from and copied other people's ideas, books, CDs, DVDs, podcasts and seminars.

I have also learned from the many successes, and also the failures, of the two and a half thousand property investors and businesspeople I have personally mentored through my 12-month mentorship program over the last 14 years. I am very proud of your successes.

And finally, to you the reader — thank you for choosing to invest in this book. Please take advantage of the information I have to offer by using it to become a better persuader so you can achieve more of what you want in life, by helping other people achieve what they're after.

Contents

INTRODUCTION: LIFE IS A SERIES OF NEGOTIATIONS

■ ■ ■

If you think about it, you've been negotiating all your life. I remember the days when I used to trade footballer cards in the playground at school (and I usually got the worse end of the deal) or exchange the sandwich my mother gave me for someone else's more appetising lunch. I didn't realise it at the time, but I was learning the art of negotiations.

It's not that different as an adult. We're negotiating with utility providers, we negotiate our salaries, whether we're buying or renting we negotiate property deals, we negotiate with friends and family and if you're a business owner you'll be negotiating with your team. Life is a series of negotiations.

Yet how many times have you felt that you should have gotten a better deal, but didn't know how to do it?

If I asked a group of people to indicate whether they enjoyed being ripped off or taken for a ride, very few people would raise their hands. But if I asked the same group whether they enjoyed landing a good deal, or bargaining successfully for what they truly want, then there would be a sea of raised hands before me.

And yet despite our love of a good deal, often we're not so great at closing one — either as the salesperson or the consumer.

More to the point: we don't have the tools or the techniques to make sure we walk away from any negotiation or transaction with the best deal possible. I know some people think we have to be aggressive or underhanded to get what we want, but this couldn't be further from the truth.

So instead of negotiating, we make do, and we make excuses. We don't get what we want, and we don't get ahead.

But you can change this once you know how.

The purpose of this book is to teach you how to get other people to *want* to do what you want them to do because your ability to interact, communicate, negotiate, influence and persuade others determines the level of your income more than most other factors.

But this book is not just for salespeople, it's for you as a consumer because, as I said, life is an ongoing series of negotiations.

In every transaction there is a buyer and a seller: they either buy what you're saying, or you buy what they're saying. Guess which side I like being on?

I want to teach you the skills to get what you want, when you want, while still retaining good relationships with friends, co-workers and customers for life.

While plenty of books teach sales and negotiation techniques, this one will explain the fundamentals and the psychology behind why the techniques work and how to use them most effectively. It's more than just a book about negotiation. It's about persuasion and influence, and more importantly, how to wield those two important traits to meet your goals.

It will change how you do business, how you interact with your family and friends and hopefully give you a greater understanding of why people behave, and are motivated to act, the way they do.

Why should you listen to me?

The truth is...I'm a Power Negotiator and for years my publisher has been encouraging me to write a book on negotiation. He argued, quite persuasively, that the lessons I have learned being directly and indirectly involved in more than $3 billion worth of property transactions spanning four decades, as well as the lessons I have learned helming a national business, would benefit others.

The more I thought about it, the more I became convinced that there was a real need for a book that clearly spelled out the kinds of techniques I have been using for decades to drive my business forward.

The skills and knowledge I'll be sharing with you have been gathered from the best of the best. I've been involved in multiple businesses over the last 40 years, and today, as CEO of the Metropole Group of companies, I regularly train and mentor our award-winning team of property strategists, wealth advisors, financial planners and real estate buyers' agents.

I have been voted Australia's leading property educator or advisor five times in the last eight years and I am the author of eight best-selling books. During my long career, I have learned that to be a successful educator you need to be a good influencer and a good persuader.

I'm not telling you all this this to brag — the truth is I'm only good at a handful of things! Just asked my wife Pam how good I am at fixing things around the house.

I have spent many years and tens of thousands of dollars studying some of the most powerful and effective persuasion experts, speakers and influencers on the planet. Over the years I've practiced what I've learned from them and after much trial and error and awkwardly trying to improve my negotiation skills my results steadily improved, my confidence grew and so did my bank account.

In turn I have become a powerful influencer and, in the process, a great salesperson, and I have helped many of my clients become wealthy, because I know the best way to become wealthy is to help other people achieve what they want. Along the way I have also taught many of my team to become power negotiators.

In fact, I remember a top salesman speaking of my persuasion skills, claiming, 'If I went into a pet shop to buy a cat and I ran into Michael Yardney, he'd probably be the only one able to convince me to walk out with a dog.'

That's not to say that how I negotiate hasn't changed over the years. I first learned about negotiation from some great masters: Herb Cohen, Zig Ziglar, Brian Tracey, Wayne Berry. But boy has the world changed since I first studied these concepts more than 30 years ago.

Back then, the paradigm was based on trusting others until they gave you a reason to do otherwise. I remember the first book I read on sales told me to spend a few minutes on building rapport, then I was told to 'disturb' the prospect, make my presentation and spend the bulk of the time handling their objections.

The old heavy-handed, pushy sales tactics I first learned to negotiate and persuade others into a sale just don't work today, especially with the younger generations. Millennials nowadays are more sceptical and more aware than ever of the presence of pushy sales tactics around them. I have heard that while ABC used to stand for 'Always be closing', now it stands for 'Always be caring'. Care first and close later.

Today the sales process has been turned on its head and it's based much more on people needing a reason to trust you first. You have to spend time getting to know your prospect or customers' wants, needs, fears and desires. To become a power negotiator, you need to understand human psychology and human nature.

Now here's a bold claim...What you'll learn from me in this book works. I know this to be true because the lessons I will teach you come from the real world, from doing lots of deals, on both sides of the ledger — as the salesperson (persuader) and the customer — and I've seen the results that my team and I have achieved. What you're going to learn from me is based on reality, not theory. Like you I need techniques that work in the real world.

Who is this book for?

At first glance it may look like this book is written for sales-people to help them improve their skills. And while that's true, it is actually for a much wider audience.

How so? Well, as I said, all of life is a negotiation, as we are always negotiating in some way.

When you walk down a busy pavement you negotiate with the others: who do you let get in front of you and when do you push in? You negotiate in all facets of your work life as well as at home. You decide who gets to choose the movie you watch on Netflix and who takes out the garbage. Who cooks the dinner that night and who chooses the holiday destination.

Whether you're discussing dinner options, seeking a pay rise or buying an investment property, most of our daily

interactions with each other involve a haggle of some kind —
subtle as it may be.

When you think about it, a large part of life is about 'I want...'
- 'I want a 10% pay increase.'
- 'I want to buy that car for no more than $30,000.'
- 'I want you to clean up your room.'

So there are very few people who would not benefit from this
book. If you do happen to **work in sales** you will, of course,
enjoy many of the concepts as you sharpen your ability to
manage one-on-one selling, as well as one-to-many selling,
such as via emails, social media or the internet.

If you **run a business** or are a **busy professional**, then this
book is also for you. Think of the lost income, the lost opportunities and the many things you've missed out on by not
being able to persuade your potential clients effectively.

And this book is also aimed at the **average consumer** dealing
with businesses they hope to buy something from, whether
it's a big-ticket item, like a property or a car, or a smaller
item as the tips in this book will help you deal with forceful
salespeople.

Think of how much extra you've paid for your home, your
investment property, your car or the many electronic goods
and appliances you've bought! Once you are aware of them,
the techniques I detail will be easily detected when salespeople try to use them on you in the future.

Ask yourself: how much will you make or save in the future when you become a better negotiator?

I know some business owners and certain professionals will start reading and say, *'This won't work for me.'* The problem is this is how most people's brains are wired. When they hear a new idea they immediately discount it by thinking it won't work for them or in their industry. On the other hand, successful people will read the same information and ask: *'How can I apply this to what I do? Are there any assumptions that I have subconsciously been using that may no longer be correct?'*

So, as you read through this book I want you to constantly ask yourself *'How can I make this work for me?'* Because whether you're on the side of the deal persuading others to buy from you, listen to you or do what you want or the other side (the consumer) you're continuously negotiating.

It's really about influence

But this book is about much more than negotiation and locking down deals — it's about persuasion and influence.

Let me explain a little about what I mean. Typically, most books, articles and blogs on negotiation teach that you have to meet half-way. That you have to give and take, find the happy middle.

But let's be honest: we don't always want to do that, do we?

So, if you want to walk away with the best deal, you're going to have to learn how to persuade others. You'll want to learn how to give a teeny bit so the other party comes over to where you are, to your point of view. For you to get what you want, you're going to have to somehow cause other people to *do* what you want.

But don't get me wrong, you still need to do the right thing by people.

The difference between manipulation and persuasion is intent. I'm not going to teach you hard sell persuasion techniques — even though what you're going to learn in this book can be used to manipulate people — but that's not my intention and I hope it's not yours!

If your intent is to sell something (be it a product or your service) to someone that they don't want, need, desire or worse, something that won't produce the outcome they want, you're a con artist.

However, if your intention is to help someone get the results they want, then I believe you should use every tool of persuasion, negotiation, influence and sales strategy to close the sale.

Why I learned about negotiation

You may be wondering why I developed such an interest in negotiation and the art of securing the best deal.

Well, let me tell you I wasn't always an expert negotiator. In fact, I let myself be manipulated one too many times when I was younger.

You see, I wasn't born into wealth. I come from a working-class immigrant family — I arrived in Australia when I was three — and we didn't have much money growing up. My parents were wonderful in that they wanted me to succeed, but they didn't have the tools to show me how.

I came to realise that my friends' parents had the right idea. While my father was an employee his whole life, my friends' parents were often running their own business and had great financial and negotiation skills.

Sometime during my teens, I decided I would be wealthy and independent like them and I wanted to be involved in real estate, impressed by the flashy cars and high-stakes deals.

Wow. Did the world see me coming! In the early years, I was a sucker when it came to persuasion and I let people sell me things I didn't want.

I knew I had to change and a major shift in my mindset occurred in the 1980s when I read the book *Influence: The Psychology of Persuasion* by Robert Cialdini.

It opened my eyes and I began to see why and how some people are good negotiators and persuaders, as well as the psychology that motivates people to make certain decisions.

I realised that to get what I wanted in life I had to somehow cause other people to do what I want them to do.

I also learned from negotiation expert Herb Cohen, who wrote in his book, *You Can Negotiate Anything*, that while some people are terrible negotiators, it's a skill that can always be learned. You may at times have felt frustrated by your inability to persuade others, your inability to get what you want. I used to feel that way too.

All of us, at some point, have been under the influence of a good negotiator. Have you ever experienced a time when you were moved to act, compelled to do something or buy something that you were prepared to do almost anything to get it? Why were you so compelled to overcome your fears and take action?

What if you could bottle that kind of power? What if you could harness this? The ability to persuade others to move through their hesitancies and act on your suggestions.

What would that power, the power to persuade, the power to influence be worth to you?

The fact that you've opened this book is a great first step. By the end of this book you will have learned the science behind influence and the techniques Power Negotiators use. When you learn to persuade others, life will become easier and you'll reach your goals — both personal and financial — much sooner. If you don't become a good negotiator your dreams will be harder to reach, and your life will seem out of control, veering from great highs to lows with the feeling that no one is behind the wheel.

Well, it's time to take control. Mastering the art of persuasion and influence is a valuable investment of your time and energy. Once you learn the fundamental skills you'll know how to communicate, what to say and when to say it so the other party 'gets it'.

As you go through your life, it won't be a question of whether or not you negotiate. The important question will be: how good a negotiator will you be?

After I finished writing this book there was still so much content left over, so I've decided to provide this to you as a bonus. You can access this now by registering your copy of this book at www.negotiateinfluencepersuade.com.

Now, let's get started!

Michael Yardney

SECTION ONE:

WHY NEGOTIATION IS THE HIGHEST PAID WORK YOU CAN FIND

*If you are a **poor** negotiator, you'll **spend** a fortune.*
*If you are a **good** negotiator, you'll **save** a fortune.*
*If you are a **great** negotiator, you'll **make** a fortune.*

How much negotiating will you do over the next 12 months? Let me start by suggesting that you'll be doing a lot more negotiating than you realise.

Are you, for example, planning on buying or selling a home or an investment property? How about upgrading your car?

Will you be indulging in a family holiday or buying consumer goods, such as a TV, phone or even taking out insurance?

There doesn't need to be a contract signed or a handshake made to ensure it is a negotiation, either. You may negotiate work hours with your co-worker or boss, a favour from a neighbour or set rules for weekly screen time limits with your children.

You see, a lot of negotiation goes on around the home, some of it quite subtle. What shows you watch and when, what you eat for dinner and how the household chores are completed (and by whom!) are all up for negotiation. And it's often a heated negotiation if you have teenagers in the house!

Just for the record…children make excellent negotiators. Have you ever noticed this?

They are dogged at getting what they want and they're skilled at trying different tactics until one works. They understand the psychology of their parents, including their weak spots, and they leverage this knowledge to maximum effect. They're also great at playing parents off against each other and will tell one parent that the other parent said 'yes' to their request, when really they said nothing of the sort.

That's why negotiations at home can often be a minefield. Ever tried to convince a teenager to spend their Saturday helping out with the chores? How about getting them to put their phone away at the dinner table?

As you can see, negotiation is a fundamental part of home and work life, but if you don't know what you're doing, you'll end up doing one of two things: engaging in lengthy battles of will that are exhausting or backing down and getting resentful.

Considering how much of your life will be consumed by negotiation over the next 12 months, it is worth looking at what it may be worth to you, both financially and emotionally, if you could become a better negotiator.

Let's take your career, for example. What would making an extra 10% in your business mean to you? What if you were involved in $100,000 worth of sales over the next year and managed to add 10% extra through expert negotiation skills? That would be worth an extra $10,000 to you.

If you are involved in $200,000 of negotiations, then a 10% increase in sales through negotiation would translate to an extra $20,000 in your pocket.

What if you finally got the courage to ask for an increase in your salary package and were able to use your new negotiation skills to raise your wage by 10%? Or 20%?

Negotiations don't take very long, but, done well, they can pay a very good rate and will be the highest paid work you will ever do. If for example, you managed to increase a buyer's offer for your service by $1,500 in a five-minute negotiation then that means you earned $300 a minute or $5 a second.

Or if it was a longer negotiation and you improved an opening offer by $10,000 over the course of an hour, well, you just made $10,000 an hour!

Now consider if you were the one coming face to face with an expert negotiator and lacked the skills to ensure you walked away with a good deal. See how expensive this could be for you!

Fact is, if you don't learn to become a good negotiator it's unlikely you'll end up rich.

Unfortunately, many people end up poorer than they want to be because they don't care enough about their money to learn to negotiate. In one of his older movies Woody Allen told us 'the greatest crime in our family was buying retail!'

I know that many people have disdain for some cultural groups who've been brought up to haggle on price or to ask for a discount, but they don't understand that's how business works.

I've found it's always worth asking for a discount. The only way you can lose is if you don't ask for it.

Only a few months ago I saved a very, very substantial sum by asking my banks for a discount on the many mortgages I have for my investment properties. They had dropped their mortgage rates for new customers in order to attract new business, so I figured, 'Why shouldn't I also benefit?' And boy did I benefit, just for asking.

But it's not only on large items. I even ask for a discount when I buy clothes. Sometimes I get 10% off, sometimes the retailer throws in a pair of socks and sometimes they just say no. But there's no harm in asking.

Of course, not all of the benefits of negotiation have to do with money. There are some great emotional side effects too: avoiding unnecessary conflict and emotional bargaining and ensuring both parties walk away feeling good.

What I'm trying show you is the importance of developing your negotiation skills and the very real difference they can make to your life.

And it's easy, if you're good at it. The good news is that all skills are able to be learned with a bit of effort, but the problem is that in some countries we've been taught not to negotiate as adults. So the first step in mastering negotiation is to get over our aversion to negotiate.

You see…somewhere along the line most of us learned that there is a set price for goods, and that meeting in the middle is preferable to coming out on top. Now, this isn't the case in all cultures. Many Asian cultures place negotiation and deal-making at the centre of what they do. They enshrine bargaining into everyday life and commerce, and to not engage in a bit of haggling is seen as an insult.

It's the complete opposite in many Western countries and, as a result, many adults have no idea where to start or what a good deal even looks like.

In a nutshell that's the purpose of this book — to teach you how to get the best deal every time, whether you're buying or selling.

By the way…much of this will be counter intuitive. You'll find a lot of negotiation, persuasion and influence has to do with understanding psychology — how we're wired as humans and how we make decisions.

You'll find out that we're not really rational.

I didn't realise this when I started studying the art of negotiation, but then I learned that being persuasive is a science and as I began to understand this my negotiation skills improved — as will yours. I learned that without understanding human psychology, using logic alone to influence others just didn't work because despite the fact that most us think we make rational decisions, in essence we tend to make most decisions emotionally and justify them rationally.

Now what you'll learn is not only based on my real world experience — I've been a student of the science of influence and persuasion for well over 30 years and I'm still learning — fortunately there's been a great body of social psychological research done which I will share with you to shorten your learning time. It definitely won't take you 30 years to become a power negotiator.

But you'll have to go through the same stages of learning I did.

I don't know about you but I enjoyed the first few *Star Wars* movies and remember a scene where Obi-Wan Kenobi and Luke Skywalker pulled up to a city with the droids in the back of their vehicle and Storm Troopers came up to them and said: 'We're looking for some droids.'

Obi-Wan Kenobi stared them in the eyes and said: 'These are not the droids you're looking for,' and the Storm Troopers replied, 'These are not the droids we are looking for' and turned away.

And it made me want to figure out why some people seem to have greater influence and greater persuasion skills than others and why they're able to get others to say yes more often and enjoy saying yes.

I saw the same thing happen when I went to trainings from Chris Howard and Tony Robbins, both personal development and life coaches, and also when I listened to speeches from influential politicians.

I realised that some people are so much better at persuading others — not just one on one — but when they're delivering their message one on many. Yet others have trouble getting their message across.

So I studied the fields of negotiation and influence, I worked on that craft, I read profusely and sought out mentors and looking back now I realise there were four levels of my progression to becoming a power negotiator, and you'll go through the same journey also. However, I plan to speed up your journey (mine took many, many years) by sharing the lessons in this book.

Here's the typical journey to learning any new skill:

1. We all start at **unconscious incompetence** — at this level you don't even know what you don't know. That's how I was when I first started learning about negotiation and influence, I didn't realise there was an art and a science to this craft.

2. The next level is **conscious incompetence** — when I was introduced to the concept of being able to be a more influential negotiator through strategic planning of the negotiation process and by using the right words to influence people, I suddenly became conscious that I was incompetent. I knew that there was a lot I didn't know. So I started to learn and moved to the next level.

3. I studied persuasion, body language and NLP and began to incorporate the lessons I learned so I became **consciously competent**. You've probably experienced this progression yourself when you learned to ride a bike or drive a car or play golf.

4. But after becoming proficient and adding another layer of learning and another, I became like Obi-Wan Kenobi — **a Jedi Knight at influence and persuasion**.

I'll help you attain the Jedi Knight level of persuasion by teaching you the many different lessons I learned. In fact, that's what the first section of this book is about. And then I'll try and pull it all together by explaining how to use these lessons in real life situations.

Let's start by understanding the typical structure and stages of a negotiation.

WHO GETS THE BIGGEST SLICE OF PIE? UNDERSTANDING THE STRUCTURE AND STAGES OF A NEGOTIATION

■ ■ ■

Now it's time to get into the nitty-gritty, the fun stuff, of negotiation theory and techniques.

It's useful to understand that there are three types of negotiations and it's useful to think of them in terms of pies. The three types are:

1. Limited pie
2. Expandable pie
3. Unlimited pie

The pie is a helpful analogy because no matter what people are negotiating over, it always seems they want the biggest slice of pie.

So, let's discuss these three types in a bit more detail.

1. LIMITED PIE

A limited pie negotiation is when there is a certain, fixed-sized pie over which both sides wrestle. One party wins and the other loses.

These are essentially one-off negotiations like buying a house, a used car or some electronic equipment (like your next smartphone) where it isn't necessary to build long-term relationships, because being in a win/lose scenario and getting more than your share of pie doesn't make for great long term relationships — does it?

The problem here is that unless you know what you're doing, you can quickly become shark bait for the other side and walk away with a smaller piece of pie than you hoped for.

2. EXPANDABLE PIE

Depending on what the pie is, you can also have an 'integrative negotiation' in which the parties can actually enlarge the size of the pie. In this instance, if both parties work well together and the relationship successfully builds and grows stronger, then both sides will benefit.

A good example of this is when a supplier and a retailer work together to improve both their bottom lines and notch up more sales. The harmonious working relationship of both sides ensures they can expand the pie for everyone.

3. UNLIMITED PIE

Then there's the unlimited pie, which takes the expandable pie concept a step further. This is the model for the ongoing relationship, whether it be with a client or in a marriage and is focused on creating opportunities for everyone.

You can see the unlimited pie model at work when bosses share their fortunes with dedicated and invested staff, or in the case of fast food tycoon, Ray Kroc, who made many of his McDonald's suppliers multimillionaires.

My suggestion is to always look for ways to make the pie bigger, because the only way to ensure that both parties end the negotiation with more than they bargained for (that often sought-after win-win) is to find more items to bring to the negotiating table.

And there are always ways to add more to the negotiation. Car salespeople are used to throwing something in to make the purchase of that expensive car seem better value. It could be free servicing, or a special protection finish on the paint or a year's insurance. What do these items cost the dealership? Well, very little compared to the price of the car.

Case Study:
Not that long ago, Peter, a minor partner of mine in a small joint venture business, approached me wanting to increase

his proportionate share of the business, offering to buy
a percentage of my share in the business.

I said, 'I guess you're looking to make more money now that
the business is working well' and of course he agreed. I told him I
was not prepared to lower my proportionate share but the easiest
way for him to make more money was to make the business more
profitable (expand the pie) and that way his share would become
more valuable and he would have extra income. While Peter was
disappointed that he didn't walk away from the negotiation with
a bigger share of the company, he was more than satisfied because
we ended up making plans to increase the profitability of the
business and in the end Peter would end up with more money
in his pocket, which after all was really what he was after.

Negotiation outcomes

If you think about it, there are only three possible outcomes
of a negotiation:

1. WIN-WIN:

The win-win situation results in both parties feeling good
about the agreement or outcome. These types of outcomes are
vital when you want to build a lasting long-term relationship.

Now, not everyone wants to play for a win-win. I'm sure
you've met someone who seems hell-bent on winning at

any cost. That doesn't mean that you can't come out on top though. The trick in this situation is to make the person *think* that they have won at your expense or that they've walked away with more than they initially hoped for.

Let's take selling a property for example. Just say you want $500,000 for your house, but you advertise it for $550,000.

You eventually sell it for $505,000 and the purchaser thinks they are in a win-lose (they won and you lost) negotiation, but in fact you achieved a better outcome than you hoped for by being tactical and keeping your cards close to your chest.

2. WIN-LOSE:

Unlike the win-win, the win-lose involves at least one party walking away with a dud deal. This happens all the time in business. Sometimes the losing party is aware that they have lost and at other times they are completely oblivious! This often happens when the losing party walks into the negotiation without a clear strategy which makes them easy prey for the other party, who is determined to win, to manipulate. It's only in hindsight, once they've left the negotiation, that they realise what they have given up.

When you're in a win-lose negotiation, it's important to make sure you know how to negotiate your way out of a bad deal and into a much better scenario. (Don't worry — I'll show you how soon.)

Sometimes 'winning' a win-lose involves walking away from a deal altogether because the person you're negotiating with is giving you no room to move. As far as I'm concerned, in this instance walking away amounts to a win.

3. LOSE-LOSE:

Now, I know what you're thinking: Why would anybody play to lose?

Let me assure you that I've found that some people would rather lose than let you win.

Sure it makes no logical sense, but as you work your way through this book, you'll come to realise that we're rarely rational with major negotiations. I've seen this on many occasions at my multi-day property workshops, where I teach negotiation and run a negotiating game in which participants are given a set of rules.

Some are buyers in the game while others are sellers, but the instructions are to complete a win-win negotiation within 15 minutes.

It's interesting that despite the fact that it is only a game, and they are given strict instructions to complete the negotiation within 15 minutes, some people just can't allow themselves to let the other party win so they end up in a lose-lose situation where they don't finalise the negotiation.

So it's important to understand this take-no-prisoners psychology that some people bring into the negotiating game.

How you handle the negotiation and how hard you'll fight for one of these outcomes will depend on whether you have a high interest or a low interest in an ongoing relationship with the other party and if you have a high interest or a low interest in the end result of the negotiation.

If you don't really like the other party, you're more likely to have a tendency to play win-lose. On the other hand, if you like the other party or you're keen to have an ongoing relationship with them, you're more likely to be lenient — even to the point of playing lose-win.

The structure of a negotiation

Now the exact structure of a negotiation depends on how complex it is. If you decide to buy an ice cream, you simply decide on what flavour you want, hand over your money and it's over in a minute or two.

On the other hand, larger negotiations go through more specific phases and to ensure they come out on top, successful negotiators apply a structure to their negotiating process. In some major negotiations some of the following stages may take days, weeks or even months to complete.

The seven stages of the negotiation process are:

1. The preparation and planning stage.
2. The building a rapport stage.
3. The gathering of information phase.
4. The probing and exploring stage.
5. The bargaining and problem-solving stage.
6. Closing and implementing the deal.
7. The finalising or nailing down phase.

Understanding these phases will empower you, while not understanding the typical stages of a negotiation can often lead to you feeling out of control and disempowered.

Most negotiations fail owing to a mistake at one of these critical stages, so it's important not to rush to stage seven — as tempting as that may be.

In larger negotiations, not only is each stage important, the order in which you work through them is vitally important. Like the steps or rungs on a ladder, if you miss a step, you may be at risk of taking a tumble.

I've seen experienced salespeople jump right into stage three, the gathering of information stage, without first establishing some rapport and therefore being shut down very quickly in the form of 'No thanks, I'm just looking!'

Similarly, I've seen salespeople move straight into the sales stage, stage six, without exploring the other party's needs and then wondering why the negotiation didn't work out.

They're too busy selling what they want to sell rather than understanding the needs of their prospect.

Without working through the stages in the right order, you may find that you're way off target with what you are recommending to your prospect. You may offer too much or not enough. You may give up some items, including price, too quickly that you should have held back.

Remember, price is not the only important factor in a negotiation. That's why stage three is of paramount importance, so you can discover what are the other important considerations for the other party. Inexperienced negotiators often assume that price is the only factor, which is why they resort to discounting too quickly. Professional negotiators may end the same encounter without hurting their bottom line at all, while at the same time ensuring that the customer walked away with an even higher level of satisfaction.

Preparation

The importance of proper preparation can't be over-stated. In his great book *Never Split the Difference*, ex FBI Hostage negotiator Chris Voss explains:

'When the pressure is on, you will not rise to the occasion, you will fall...to your highest level of preparation.'

Now you're probably not negotiating for people's lives, but many people you will negotiate with will behave as if their lives depend on it (because their livelihood does). Yet most people walk into negotiations having done insufficient preparation and as a result they're out of their depth. Good preparation is simple, everyone can do it, but very few people take the time out of their day to actually do it. But what a difference it makes!

Let me take you through a preparation checklist that will make it easy for you to be across the details come negotiation time.

1. What is your bottom line?

In other words: how high are you prepared to go if you're buying and how low are you prepared to go if you're selling? If you're not negotiating money, and it's chores or your kids' homework that is the issue at hand, then let's call your version of the bottom line your Lowest Acceptable Position (LAP).

Now you may think having worked out your bottom line is common sense, but you have no idea how many people I've seen enter a negotiation on buying a house, or making other expensive purchases without an absolute set limit in mind as to what they're willing to pay. This ensures that they make an emotional purchase rather than a financial one, often to their detriment.

2. What is your best scenario outcome?

In negotiating circles, your ultimate outcome is referred to as your Highest Advanced Position (HAP)— essentially, the *most* you feel you could ask for and get.

As a buyer, this is the *lowest* possible price that you feel you may be able to pay and still get what you want, whereas for sellers, it's the highest possible price that you feel you can ask for that will be accepted. In negotiations, you need to keep as close to your HAP as possible, and as far away from your LAP as is prudent. You may need to build in some concessions to your planning that you would be prepared to make and that you feel would be important to the other party.

The following diagram illustrates the concepts of LAP and HAP:

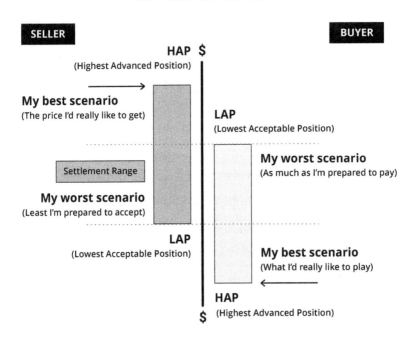

SETTLEMENT RANGE

Once you have established *both* your LAP and your HAP — they are equally important, so you need both — the gap in between is what is known as your *negotiating range*, essentially your high point and your low point.

Now that you have formulated your Best Scenario Position, you need to steam ahead with your preparations.

3. Clarify your real objectives

It's important to be absolutely clear about what your **must-haves** are, as this can prevent you from accepting something as a 'win' that you never even wanted to begin with. It's also important to have an **'intend to have'** list that make up the ideal outcome scenario you would like to have, but they are not absolutely essential. Similarly, your **'nice to have'** list is made up of outcomes or items that are not a deal-breaker but would be the cherry on top.

Do your best to anticipate what the other party's objective might be. Just as it's important to consider what your 'must haves', 'nice to haves' and 'intent to haves' are, it's important to consider the other person's may be. Ask yourself what they are seeking and what they are motivated by. What is their HAP and LAP?

In a big negotiation it is worth writing all of this down so you can determine, as much as possible, what their negotiating range may be. You can then compare your negotiating range with what you anticipate the negotiating range of the other party to be, and if they overlap you have reached a possible settlement range — an area where both parties may get some of what they want.

The greater the overlap, the greater the chance both negotiating parties will come out happy. If there is no overlap, then it's unlikely both sides will be catered to, unless the negotiating range can be negotiated further.

Where you can see differences, ask yourself how great the conflict is. How could you create a win-win here?

4. Look behind the words
While you're in the other person's shoes and determining where the common ground and conflict may be, it's worth digging a little deeper. In order to succeed in negotiations, you need to understand what the other party *really* wants. It's not always about the money or the product or service that is being negotiated. It could be that they want to feel that you have given some ground, or that they are being heard. That is why creating the feeling that the other party has won is hugely important.

5. What if it fails?
No one goes into a negotiation expecting it will fail, but top negotiators have plans in case it does fail. Psychologically, this puts them in a very strong position. You want to negotiate a good deal, but if it falls over you have prepared for that scenario. Think of the worst (realistically) thing that will happen if the negotiation falls over and you're likely to realise it's not that bad and that you have alternatives.

6. What will you discuss?
A negotiation shouldn't be a free-for-all discussion of all the relevant issues. Smart negotiators know what to discuss and when.

For example, let's say you're negotiating an upgrade to your room at a hotel. You've politely requested the upgrade to the premium club suite and after staff have checked the room is available and they are able to grant this request, the upgrade is agreed to.

Once the keys are being arranged, it's then time to confirm the club suite privileges, by stating towards the end of the transaction: 'Of course, the room comes with the usual club suite privileges, doesn't it?' The person is much more likely to say 'yes' at this point than if you had of bundled the request into the beginning of the conversation by asking for an upgrade, as well as the hotel's club privileges. It's called nibbling, and it's a highly effective technique (but it's a nuisance when used against you!).

7. Consider the timeframe

Time pressures can work for or against you, so make sure you consider the timeframe of the negotiation and how it impacts on yourself and the other party. If the other party is facing time pressures, then you can obviously use this to your advantage.

In a future chapter I'll explain how the more time the other party has invested in the negotiation, the more concessions they are likely to give up to you. This is because in the back of their mind they are subconsciously thinking, 'Geeez, since I have spent so much time and gone this far on this deal, it won't hurt giving up these minor concessions.'

8. *The opening positions*

Jot down some of your opening positions and what demands or requests you will put forward. What is your opening strategy? What demands is the opening party likely to put forward? What will your counter response to those be?

Make sure you consider the concessions you're willing to make too, and what the cost of these concessions would be to you (whether they are worth making). What concessions will you ask for in return?

Remember, concessions should not be made just for the sake of it if the cost is too high. It's always worth having some requests that you are not expecting to receive or are of no real value to you as 'concessions' that you can give up, allowing you to stand firm on what is of value to you. Keep in mind that when you reciprocate a concession given to you, never give away a concession that is perceived to be greater in value.

9. *Know the other negotiator*

If you're undertaking a major negotiation it's fundamentally important to know as much as you can about the other negotiating party, prior to your meeting. Google is a treasure trove of information, and can unearth company reports, statements, and media articles about the person and their company. You can also chat to industry insiders and people who have worked with the other negotiating party previously to get a real sense for what makes them tick, and what their wants and needs are.

If you're meeting a group of people, make sure you know who the decision-maker of the group is, and go as far as possible in ensuring that the person who will approve the final deal is in the room.

It's also worth determining what their negotiation style is likely to be. Will they be cool, calm and collected, saying very little and attempting to give you enough rope to hang yourself? Will they yell and scream to try and intimidate you? Or will they be disarmingly friendly? You need to consider all possibilities, as well as your possible reaction to each style. Will you react positively to their behaviour or play hard ball yourself? Which style suits you best?

To get a real feel for all potential outcomes, role play some scenarios with a colleague or friend, or at least in your mind, to help you prepare for all negotiation styles.

10. Am I shooting myself in the foot?

I have seen this time and time again: a negotiator holds firm on a position for short-term gain, but long-term loss. For example, imagine I have a dispute over a small charge that I don't believe I should have paid. A smart business would reimburse the charge, because while it may cost them in the short term, they will be rewarded in the long run as I will keep using their services and contribute much more financially over the coming years.

11. Lawyer up?

When signing an important contract, it is always worth

seeking legal advice if this is new terrain to you.

12. Finally, question your assumptions

Go back over your notes and look at where you've made assumptions and ask yourself whether these are accurate. What if your assumptions turn out to be wrong? How would his affect the negotiation?

The final assumption to analyse is the one you may be making about yourself. Are you really the best person to conduct the negotiation? Maybe you are, or maybe you're too emotionally attached to the deal, especially if you're buying or selling a home.

Even the best negotiators can come undone if they're too emotionally invested. So be smart and know when it's time to pull yourself out of the negotiation for the sake of the deal. Otherwise, you could end up making a very expensive mistake.

What's next?

In the next few chapters I'm going to summarise many of the lessons I learned from my teachers and mentors about the psychology and science behind human behaviour. Understanding these principles will help you better influence others.

Then we'll look into some practical applications of these lessons.

DO YOU ENJOY NEGOTIATING AND SELLING?

For you to become a power negotiator you're going to have to become comfortable with negotiating and if you're in sales, to be successful you must feel good about selling — whether it's selling goods, services, your professional services or just your expertise.

In fact, you're going to have to become a top salesperson.

Now even if your job description doesn't include 'sales', this chapter is still for you as in reality we're all in 'sales' because we're continuously negotiating in all aspects of our lives and while you may not be selling products or services, you're selling your ideas, like what you want your spouse to do, or how you want your children to behave.

So, read on and you'll learn some ideas and insights into how top salespeople and negotiators think.

Time for a little confession…

When I first started out, I didn't enjoy sales. I didn't have any training for it, and I felt I shouldn't have to 'sell' my

ideas or concepts. I knew they were right for my clients.
I knew how to create wealth through property. I had
achieved it and I felt that my potential clients should
believe me.

Boy I was naïve back then.

But, as I increased my skills, like you're doing now by reading
this book, and the more comfortable I became with selling,
my thinking changed. I began to realise that your mindset is
a major factor in how well you persuade or influence others
and how well you negotiate.

I knew the services we provided for our clients at Metropole
helped them become financially fluent and build a property
portfolio which would help them become financially free.
And as I increased my skills, selling became fun and I started
making more money, which was obviously enjoyable. And I
was helping more people, so over time my thought patterns
actually changed.

Today I enjoy influencing and persuading people. I really
enjoy selling whether it is one on one as I consult with
the few high net worth clients I see (I'm at the stage of my
career where I no longer see many clients) or when I get on
stage and influence hundreds of people.

Way back one of my friends Thomas Beck taught me something that changed my outlook on business he said: *You can*

get all you want in life if you just help enough other people get what they want.'

Now, I know you've probably heard this dozens of times, but it directly applies to professional selling, which is really helping your prospects get what they want. It is helping them get out of pain and move into pleasure, it is helping them solve a problem that they have, it is helping them get an outcome that they want to achieve that they cannot get on their own without your help.

If you look at selling this way, it will give you a different perspective.

You see…selling is not about tricking people. It's about helping people, and the more people that you help, the more money you make, and when you do it in a sophisticated, non-threatening, non-salesy way, your prospects or clients will love the process and the experience with you.

I'm going to ask you a couple of questions, so please answer these questions honestly for yourself.

The reason I'm doing this is to make you realise that successful selling, persuading or influencing is a transfer of emotion.

That means how you feel about your product, how you feel about your service and more importantly, how you feel about 'selling' your product or service affects how your prospects feels about your product or service.

Now you probably understand that how you feel about your product or service affects how your prospect will feel, but you may have missed a little subtlety. How you feel about *selling* your product or service also affects how your prospect feels.

You see, if you feel uncomfortable selling your emotion, your energy, that feeling is going to come across to your prospect. If they feel you're not confident, if they feel you don't truly believe in what you're saying, that is going to negatively impact your ability to influence them or negotiate a deal.

On the other hand, if you're passionate about what you're trying to persuade the other party to do, your enthusiasm will transfer to them.

So, here are the questions I'd like you to answer. It's not going to help if you fool yourself or you trick yourself or give the answer that you think should be the answer. You need to dig deep and answer these questions honestly to yourself.

1. Do you enjoy selling?
Interestingly I've found that many business owners and most professionals don't like selling. If you think like this, you'll never become a top influencer or negotiator.

2. Do you believe that selling is an honourable profession?
I know many people believe that sales in a dishonest business where you're trying to trick someone into buying something.

Now I understand why. Many of us believe salespeople are sleazy and just trying to coax people into buying things they don't really need, using slick sales techniques to force the person into buying.

If you're in sales as a professional I'm sure that's not how you want to come across.

So, for you to be successful in sales, for you to become a persuasive influencer and a top negotiator you'll need to genuinely believe that selling is a noble profession, and that you're helping your prospect, not tricking them. You're not forcing them to do anything that they don't want to do or that isn't good for them.

If you've ever sat with me in a strategic property consultation, you'll know I absolutely believe in the recommendations I make for my clients so I'm passionate about my suggestions, and this excitement transfers to them.

3. Do you believe that Selling is one of your most important jobs?
I find that, 'I shouldn't have to sell' is the thought process of many people, especially those with professional degrees like doctors, dentists, lawyers.

They tend to believe they shouldn't have to sell — that selling is somehow beneath them.

After all they've got these 'qualifications' and because they're good at what they do people should just buy from them or use their services.

But, if you're in business or a professional the truth is that selling is one of your most important jobs, and even if you are currently an employee — becoming good at sales is one of the fastest ways up the pay ladder — good salespeople are amongst the top paid professionals.

4. Do you believe you provide a superior product or service?

If you believe that you offer a better service, product or experience than your competitor then it's your moral obligation to provide that to your prospect.

But, how much passion do you have believing that your prospect must have what you're offering? It's not that they should have it, not that would be nice for them to have it, but that they *must* have it.

I passionately believe that holistic property and wealth advisory services offered by my team at Metropole are second to none. Other companies provide some of the services we do, but there is no company that I am aware of in Australia that provides the same range of services nationally. I passionately believe that those prospects who approach us and have a need for services should not go elsewhere because we provide a superior range of independent advice.

I mean, I ardently believe this. I genuinely feel if they go elsewhere they're making a mistake and taking an unnecessary risk. And my passion clearly comes across, because when I see clients face-to-face my conversion rate (a reflection of my ability to influence, persuade and negotiate) is very high.

What is the level of your belief? What is the level of your passion?

Yes...but!

I hear you...what if you sell commodities like electronic appliances or you're a professional like a dentist — you may think 'My competitors sell the same "thing" that I sell, so I don't offer a superior product or service.'

Now if that's the way you think, if you can't tell me why I should buy your product or service instead of going elsewhere, then there's no way you're going to be able to effectively persuade me to work with you.

Think about it...you're an estate agent wanting to sell people's homes or maybe you are offering financial planning services or maybe you are a doctor who's basically providing similar services to hundreds of other professionals, your prospects *should* 'buy' from you because you're going to provide superior service or you're the very best at what you do.

But to effectively persuade people to do this you'll have to truly believe on a level that is probably beyond what you're currently thinking that you offer a superior quality of service or experience or you deliver better results that anyone else, because in great part, selling, persuading or influencing is a transference of emotion and if you don't have that emotion, that belief, that confidence, then you are not going to be the effective influencer you could be.

Now I think it's unlikely you'll be in your particular job if you don't truly believe in it. Think about how you have changed people's lives, how you've impacted people's lives. Read through some testimonials your clients have sent you or look at the results you've achieved or the people whose lives you have impacted.

Rekindle your passion, and if you can't achieve a sincere level of passion, then maybe you should consider it's time to be working in different field, selling something else.

As I said in the beginning of this chapter, your belief in what you're selling, what you're try to persuade somebody to do is critical do your success. Just think about some of impassioned orators that have moved you like Martin Luther King's famous 'I've got a Dream' speech.

It's the same for negotiating

Let me ask you another question: how do you really feel about negotiating?

If you grew up in a Western country you've probably been brought up to instinctively avoid negotiating.

Imagine you wanted to buy a new television and the price tag in the store says *'Special: Was $2,500 — Now $1,995.'*

Most people would say 'Wow, what a bargain' and pay $1,995.

Let's shift this scene to an Asian country — this time you grew up in China, India or Vietnam. Do you pay $1,995? I bet you don't — because culturally you know that price tag is the beginning of a negotiation, not the end point.

I hope by the time you finish this book you'll end up with a different view of negotiation. You'll see opportunities to negotiate all around you — ones that you didn't recognise before. And you'll feel good about taking advantage of these opportunities and negotiating the best deal for yourself.

The main message I'm trying to get across in this chapter is that for you to become a power negotiator, before you learn any new sales techniques or fancy scripts, you must work on your mindset and your thoughts. Only then will your level of influence increase.

I've said it before, but this point is so important I'll repeat it. If you're in sales, a business person or a professional, you can get everything that you want by helping more customers, more clients, more patients get what they want and the only way to do that is to embrace selling as something noble because that is exactly what it is.

But becoming an expert in persuasion is going to take a lot more that confidence in your product or service or professional offering. You're going to have to understand the needs of your prospects and learn how they communicate and how to communicate effectively with them. That's what I'm going to be discussing in the next few chapters.

UNDER THE (INVISIBLE) INFLUENCE

■ ■ ■

Some people are very good at getting what they want. This is rarely down to good fortune — although a little luck doesn't hurt — but more to do with their skills in persuasion. Somehow they have mastered the skills needed to convince other people to do exactly what they want.

They've achieved this not by force or threats — that is the exact opposite of the art of persuasion — but by using their ability to convincingly advocate for exactly what they want or need, while keeping everyone happy. Particularly proficient negotiators are even be able to convince you that the outcome that suits them was your idea!

When dealing with such top-notch negotiators, you may feel as if there is some kind of charm to their ability to persuade you. While it may seem like they possess a kind of magic touch, in reality, what they're doing has a highly scientific basis.

While you may think that you don't have the gift of the gab or the people skills to win others over, what you probably lack is knowledge of the tried-and-tested methods that I've learned and have now been using for decades. I have seen both extroverts and introverts alike, become highly proficient negotiators once they applied themselves consistently to truly master this art.

As I explained I've spent a lot of time studying the science behind persuasion because I realise that if you can persuade other people, the world is your oyster. People are time poor these days; they don't have hours upon hours to consider all the research you put before them. They need someone to condense and advocate the best path forward, and they want decisions made for them by people they trust.

This is where you will come in.

One of my most influential mentors in the field of negotiation was Dr. Robert Cialdini, a professor of psychology and marketing. His classic book *Influence: The Psychology of Persuasion* is a must read for all salespeople and has greatly influenced all the marketing and sales techniques my team and I employ, so I'd like to unpack his work for you.

Following many years of studying why some people are more persuasive than others Cialdini boiled it down to six principles of influence:

1. RECIPROCITY

The concept of reciprocity has been around for millions of years. It is a behavioural pattern that has helped us survive as human beings.

You know... 'I'll scratch your back if you scratch mine.'

And it if you want to become a power negotiator then you'll need to employ the principle which says that if someone performs a favour for you, such as giving you a gift, doing you a favour or inviting you to a party, then you will feel obliged to repay them.

As humans we feel a strong social obligation to return the favour. It's hardwired into our psychology and you could even argue this kind of obligation is important for a fully functioning society.

The best way to illustrate this concept is through a study on reciprocity that looked at the tipping habits of people depending on whether they were given a sweet or a mint with their bill.

The 2002 study by the Cornell University School of Hotel Administration was conducted in a small restaurant with some diners given candy, while others weren't.

All up, 46 participants received a bill with mints and the other 46 participants received none. The results showed that the average tip for people who received the candy was 17.8% compared to an average tip of 15.1% without candy.

A further study added another layer of human psychology. This particular study involved the giving of mints and found that giving a mint increased the tips by 3%, which chimes with the previous study. But things get really interesting when you up the ante.

The study found that tips actually quadrupled when two mints are provided. Furthermore, if the waiter provides one mint, starts to walk away from the table, turns back and says, 'For you nice people, here's an extra mint,' tips increase by 23%. That is the power of reciprocity in action and shows that *how* you give determines the amount you receive in turn.

There are three factors that will make the principle of reciprocity even more effective for you:

- *Offer something first* — this makes the other party feel indebted to you
- *Offer something exclusive* — this makes them to feel special
- *Personalise the offer* — which makes sure they know it's from you

2. SCARCITY

The scarcity principal operates on the premise that people want more of those things they can have less of. They place greater value to things that are scarce.

If people think that what you're offering is commonplace and can easily be replaced, you'll struggle to persuade them to engage with your goods or services — whatever they may be. On the other hand, scarcity is a major motivator in our decision making to purchase and when you understand this it puts you in a strong position to be able to sell your services on what is unique — and not easily replicated — elsewhere.

There are two easy techniques to create scarcity.

The first is the 'limited number' technique which works because it creates added value to a product by reducing its availability. The other is the 'deadline technique' which works because it puts a time limit on the product availability.

Of course scarcity is the reason so many companies use the term 'limited edition'. As soon as someone thinks that they may not be able to buy a product or consume a service, they're suddenly banging down the door.

Cast your mind back a few decades to those Boxing Day sales that major department stores used to hold. This was the time before mid-year sales, Black Friday Sales or even online shopping, so people waited until Boxing Day to snap up some major bargains on electrical equipment. The result? An absolute stampede. People would queue for hours before the stores opened and once the doors opened, people would almost trample each other to death to reach the cut-price fridges.

There were even a few instances where people got hurt, so keen were punters to nab a bargain. Once again: that scarcity factor, the 'for one-day-only' psychology, was at work.

Another form of scarcity is what is unique about your product or service compared to your opposition. Emphasise what makes you unique, but be careful: everyone is claiming to be 'unique' these days, so you need to show it and describe how, rather than just say that you're unique or different.

This means you need to display what gives you the edge in your marketing material and in the way you talk to people. It could be your years in the industry, your different methodology or the fact that you're the only person qualified in your area to do what you do.

People need to not only realise, but really feel that should they take their business elsewhere they will get an inferior experience because what you do or what you bring is not easily found.

Are you wondering how you can use scarcity in your business? Maybe you could use these methods:

- *Limited-number* — items, services or products are in short supply and won't be available once it runs out.
- *Limited-time* — item or a special price will only available during that time period.
- *One-of-a-kind Specials* — this kind of uses one or both of the above techniques but in the form one-off events such as anniversaries or special occasions
- *Competitions* — we tend to want things more because other people also want them — by the way this principle is one of the reason property auctions work so well.

However, keep in mind to be authentic with the 'limited time' element of the offer. I have seen numerous instances of this concept backfire when retailers have been known to offer a 'limited time' offer, stop it at its expiry, only to re-offer something similar at a predictable interval in the future. Once this happens, their customers sense this and think 'It's ok if I miss out this time, because the same offer will be made available again in two months' time'.

One of my favourite restaurants has the habit of texting clients with special deals 'for that night only' when they're having a quiet night. I get at least one or two of these offers each month. When I lasted visited the restaurant, I asked the owner 'how's business?' He moaned that while he's busy, it's mostly at a lower profit margin as most of his patrons wait for the special offers and only come in then. No wonder when they know the 'special limited offer' will be back again next week.

As a purchaser, you can also use the principle of scarcity in reverse to get an upper edge...

Example: When buying a used car.

'Please remind me again, what were the extras you were offering with this car? I've been talking to so many other car dealers this week that sometimes all the deals blur together.'

Example: Hiring a builder.

'May I ask your question? If you were me talking to at all the many builders out there who are scrambling to get this job, why would you choose your company over all the others?'

3. AUTHORITY

There is a very good reason that judges wear long robes and doctors wear white coats. It imbues them with authority and places the community at ease that these pillars of the community know what they're doing (sometimes they do, sometimes they don't, but that's a topic for another time!).

Cialdini's research shows that as humans we look to signs and signifiers of authority because it's easier to trust an authority figure in a particular field than it is to do your own research on the topic.

You can see this principle used a lot in online marketing with headlines and blog posts that include phrases like 'experts say', 'research shows', or 'scientifically proven'.

In an ideal world, people would judge others on their skill and ability alone. But that's not how we are wired. We tend to form quick, split-second judgments on a person's competence based on how they dress, talk and how professional they are. Or appear to be.

It may not seem fair but research shows (see how I used the Principle of Authority) that taller and more attractive people are viewed as more trustworthy. Now, that doesn't mean short people can't get ahead. But it does mean that we should be aware of how people sub-consciously look for superficial signs of authority.

In his book Cialdini covers three factors that trigger the authority principle:

1. *Titles* — words like Dr., Prof., Ph.D., President, Chairman, Founder, CEO, Industry experts
2. *Clothes* — Uniforms like those worn by police officers, monks, nuns, priests etc.
3. *Trappings* — Accessories that go along with certain positions like expensive suits, nice cars, police badges etc.

Do you know what else helps? Referrals. People trust others — particularly if they know them — to refer people their way. How many times have you been asked whether your accountant was any good? When you renovated your kitchen, did you blindly call a builder or did you ask your friends and family for recommendations?

An authoritative referral is potent stuff. And funnily enough sometimes it doesn't matter who gives the referral — it could even be a related party. There is a great example of a real estate agency that started touting their agents' skills when prospects phoned up. So, for example, when someone asked to be put through to sales, the receptionist responded with, 'Sure, I will put you through to James in sales, who has 15 years' experience selling in this area.'

The result was that the expert introduction led to a 20% rise in the number of appointments and a 15% rise in the number of signed contracts.

Here's another great example of using authority... I recently had a problem with my computer and took it to the Apple store and received tech support at the Genius Bar. While I doubt all the staff are certified geniuses in a psychological sense, they are definitely well trained by Apple and I trust them.

What can you do to increase your perceived authority?

Get creative and think of a number of different ways you can incorporate expert introductions into you work life (without being too cheesy). You may reward satisfied customers for referring a new prospect that leads to a sale or contract. Or you could ensure your business signature has your full qualifications after your name — especially if these are hard-won or rare in your field. Even better: ask for others to refer you, as there is plenty of evidence to suggest that a third-party referral is the most effective approach.

Whatever the approach, it's important to find ways of presenting yourself as an 'authority' because very few people will take advice from, or do business, with those they don't trust.

4. COMMITMENT AND CONSISTENCY

How do you earn the loyalty of people who don't quite trust you yet?

The fastest way I know is to use principle of Commitment and Consistency.

As Professor Cialdini puts it: 'Once we have made a choice or taken a stand, we will encounter personal and interpersonal pressures to behave consistently with that commitment. Those pressures will cause us to respond in ways that justify our earlier decision.'

In other words, we feel an automatic compulsion to stick with the decision they've already made. The reason this works is because of the mental shortcut we all use to simplify our decision-making.

You see… we are given so many choices and decision to make daily, so commitment and consistency makes our lives easier by reducing the amount of things we have to think about. We just make a single decision and use that as reference for subsequent related choices. Also, we tend to view consistency as an attractive social trait.

But commitments made in private are easy to break, so it's even better if you can get your prospects to tell others because when something that we said is heard by others, there is a strong desire to want to uphold that statement.

I know I most Monday mornings I decide this is the week I'm going to start my diet, but if I tell my wife Pam about my commitment, it's harder for me to break my diet. We do that because we all feel an innate social pressure to be consistent, something known as normative social influence.

As a business owner here are three ways to leverage off this principle:

- *Ask your customers to take small steps first* — they're more likely to stick with you. Once customers can be nudged into making seemingly insignificant choices, it paves the way for you to offer them bigger choices which might be met with lesser resistance because of the first small choice that they've made.

Sales people commonly call this the 'Foot-in-the-door' technique: where a small request paves the way for compliance with larger subsequent requests.

Here's how this could work... Just say you are interested in trialling an online, at-home exercise program. You've never done anything like this before, and the prospect of paying for a 12-month subscription seems daunting.

But just say the company that is providing the exercise program offers you a 'taste test'. You can trial the program for free, or at a reduced rate, with a beginner program that is not as arduous. Chances are you will take up the offer, and if the trial goes well, continue on with the program once the trial is up.

Why? Because when approached incrementally, the program doesn't seem as intimidating, and furthermore it is also a continuation on past behaviour and humans enjoy consistency.

- *Encourage public commitments* — they'll be less likely to back out.
- *Reward your customers* for investing time and effort in your brand. You can use this to your advantage by reminding people that they are committed to you. You need not do this is a brash or explicit way, but you can offer perks or opportunities through various communication channels that really reinforce this relationship.

Because once that relationship is forged, people need a very good reason to walk away. For example, if you have a blog attached to your business, you could offer people the chance to sign up to your daily, weekly or monthly insights. By pinging into your prospects' inboxes on a regular basis, that commitment is consistently reinforced.

Here's a tip, whether you're a consumer or the salesperson: Experienced salespeople know how to use this principle of Commitment and Consistency by eliciting a series of small commitments in the form of many harmless 'Yeses' upfront and throughout the sales process. For instance, after you explain to the prospect the credibility of your company, you ask, 'Does this sound like the kind of reputable company that you want to work with?' And then a little while later, you ask another question, 'Do you want to be among the top 5% of our clients who achieve X after using our products and services?' They understand that this technique works at a subconscious level as you gradually condition the prospect's mind into making a series of small commitments through these many spoken 'Yeses'. This will eventually make them more receptive to the eventual goal of engaging your company's services (or buying your company's products).

5. SOCIAL PROOF

Not only are we creatures of habit or consistency, we're also highly social animals and this has vast ramifications for negotiators because we take our cues as to what is worthy or of value from other people, especially people we trust or people who are like us.

It's true: no matter how independently minded you may think you are, deep down you're likely to take into account other people's opinions and be influenced by reviews, testimonials and endorsements.

And in today's age of social media this principle is more important than ever, so it's a critical one to understand if you're on the selling side of the negotiation (as you should be using social proof in your marketing and your conversations with clients) or on the buying side (so you understand how you may be influenced into making decisions by power negotiators).

Just look at Twitter, Facebook or Instagram. Have you ever wondered how those social media influencers have gotten to be so... well influential?

It's because of this principle of social proof. People are more likely to 'trust' these influencers because they have tens of thousands of followers and all those other people can't be wrong — can they?

Yes… we're likely to buy a product or service or to perform a certain behaviour that has been endorsed by a person we trust, whether it's friends, family, or a celebrity.

In fact, sometimes we don't even have to know the people who are endorsing the product or service. A great example is restaurants. How likely are you to enter an empty one? Not very. How about the bustling one with only a couple of spare tables? I bet you'd walk right in. I've even heard stories of restaurants hiring crowds to line up outside their venue so people will want to come in.

And it's true: as soon as you see a line, you become intrigued as to what is so enticing.

So how can you harness this principle?

You could draw on the statistics, the happy customers, the overwhelming evidence of your market success, to really drive home the value that you bring. And when you're negotiating, it's worth using statements such as 'I've found that most people...' or 'The most common approach is...' to angle your prospect in the right (and popular) direction.

Then think about the many ways you could tap into the influence of social proof from:

- *Clients* — Public approval from past clients is critical today. There's no such thing as a blind date anymore — prospective customers do their homework online before approaching you. But your potential customers don't care about you. They want to know what other people's experiences have been with you. They're doing it for travel (Trip Advisor), they're doing it for restaurants, they're doing it for most businesses (Google reviews).
- *Experts* — Can you get the endorsement of credible experts in your field?
- *Celebrities* — What about approval or endorsements from celebrities or sports people? They may already be your customers or clients, or you may have to pay for their support.

Social pressure is a powerful force and no one wants to be the outlier who is doing things differently and missing out on all the fun and opportunity.

6. THE LIKING PRINCIPLE

The final principle is an obvious one: we like dealing with people who we like.

Think about it... We tend to believe that a person we like are trustworthy, otherwise we wouldn't like them, would we?

While people we like tend to have the similar beliefs, interests and language as we do, they can range from our closest friends to complete strangers that we are attracted to.

Skilled negotiators understand the tremendous impact the Liking Principle has on how we make decisions recognising we are more likely to comply with requests made by people that we like.

In his book Dr. Cialdini lists five factors that powers the principle of Liking:

1. *Physical attractiveness* — Good looks suggest other favourable traits such as honesty and trustworthy (yes, we do judge a book by its cover).
2. *Similarity* — We like people similar to us in terms of interests, opinions, personality, background, etc. I'll explain how you can use this principle in much more detail in an upcoming chapter.
3. *Compliments* — We love to receive praises and tend to like those who give it to us.
4. *Contact and Cooperation* — We feel a sense of commonality when working with others to fulfil a common goal.
5. *Conditioning and Association* — Associate your brand with the same values that you want to communicate and possess.

If you're wondering if this principle applied to e-commerce where you don't meet your clients face to face, the answer is yes it does. Here's how:

- *Physical attractiveness* — Make your website have the look and feel that would attract your target market.

- *Similarity* — Behave like a friend online, not a brand. On social media show others that you can relate to and understand them. Today it's critical to have a social media presence on sites like Facebook and Instagram but engage with your audience and potential customers in a more informal, friendly manner — don't be salesy!
- *Compliments* — Use social media to have conversations and form relationships with your potential customers.
- *Contact and Cooperation* — Fight for the same causes as your customers. Nothing builds rapport and closeness like good old-fashioned teamwork.
- *Conditioning and Association* — Associate your brands with the same values that you want to communicate and possess.

Building Trust

Nine-five per cent of persuasion occurs at a subconscious level. Why do we trust some people and not others?

To become influential, to persuade someone or do business with them you have to go through a number of stages — Know, Like, Trust. People have to know you; they need to like you and then to do business with you they need to trust you.

Following on from Dr Cialdini's concepts of building influence I'd like to share some ideas about building trust quickly.

Trust is the belief that someone's speech and actions will be congruent — they will speak the truth, walk their talk and follow through with their commitments. After all that's what we're looking for if we're involved in a major negotiation, isn't it?

Trust is a major ingredient in generating influence with another person — possibly the single most important. Without trust, there is little or no basis for engaging in agreements — especially when there are significant stakes involved. Trust is one of those characteristics that takes time to develop and demonstrate to others, but only takes a moment to destroy.

Kurt Mortensen, a highly regarded authority on influence and persuasion, outlined five critical components that develop trust — each of them begins with a C:

1. *Character.*— Your integrity, honesty and reputation should speak for themselves. You should also show sincerity. One way of doing this is to show a little weakness, discuss a flaw in yourself, your product or service. Doing this can turn a shortcoming into a strength because you've been honest. On the other hand, we don't trust those we perceive as lacking in character or bad mouthing their competitors.

2. *Competence.* You need to come across as capable, skilled and have the required knowledge. We don't trust those we perceive as being incompetent.

3. *Confidence.* We don't trust those we perceive as not being confident in their role or their words. So the other party should feel confident that you know what you're talking about as well as your belief in your product or service. People want to be convinced that you can help them.

4. *Credibility.* Here's where your past track record is important. We don't trust those we perceive as not being credible and today most of us use social media, Google reviews or sites like Trip Advisor to do our homework *before* the negotiation even starts. Your track record is out in the open — I guess there are no blind dates anymore.

5. *Congruence.* Do your words match your actions? We don't trust those we perceive as not being congruent in their speech and behaviour.

It's important to understand that in general in today's society we tend to look if these components are missing more than we look for their presence. Additionally, it is very easy for trust to be destroyed with one small sign or suspicion of deficiency in any one component. You need to display all five C's.

Of course, trust and the five C's are a matter of 'perception' of the other person (or our own when considering other people we're dealing with) and may have little to do with reality. That's why these early chapters in my book are teaching you about the importance of the psychological aspects of negotiation and persuasion.

David Ogilvy once said, 'People don't think what they feel, they don't say what they think, and they don't do what they say.'

The Bottom Line

It's important to realise that not only are Professor Cialdini's Six Principles of Influence incredibly powerful in their own right, but they can be combined in many ways to achieve a win-win outcome. It may take you a while to master each one, but pretty soon they will feel like natural tools in the negotiation process, assisting to becoming a powerful communicator.

In the next chapter I'm going to teach you about the different personality types, because unless you understand how people 'tick', how they communicate and how they think, you'll never be able to persuade them.

NEGOTIATING WITH DIFFERENT PERSONALITIES

■ ■ ■

One of my biggest breakthroughs as a manager and as a salesperson came when I learned that we are all different in how we perceive others, how we hear things, how we buy things and, crucially, how we negotiate.

You've probably heard about behavioural types before, but please read this chapter carefully as understanding how important this is will make a significant difference to how you persuade and influence people.

When I really understood the significance of this, it added an extra degree of sophistication and refinement to my sales process as well as improving my influence with my team at Metropole. It made me a better manager because I became an expert at adapting my conversational style to suit who I was talking to.

Now I don't need to tell you that we're all different.

In fact, I often jokingly say we're all unique and different, just like everyone else!

You've probably also noticed that we like to communicate differently and in this chapter I will outline why this is so.

You may be thinking: why even bother? Why do I need to understand other people's communication style?

The answer is so that you can build rapport with people you will be negotiating and communicating with, or in some way trying to influence or persuade.

Just to make things clear, building rapport is anything we do to maximise sameness and minimise the difference between us and others.

Remember in the last chapter I explained how we like people who are like us and we like doing business with people who are like us. It's human nature. Dealing with people you like decreases your stress levels, while increasing your levels of trust. You feel comfortable and relaxed.

Over the years I have seen many models of the different behavioural styles, but the one I would like to share with you is one I learned from American author Tony Alessandra.

He explained that there were a number of observable characteristics that would help you to define what style of person you were dealing with and the way that they like to communicate, so you can communicate with them in a manner to make them feel comfortable.

The first thing to look for, and something that is easy to recognise, is **pace**. Is someone fast paced or slow paced?

Some people speak very fast and these types also tend to be quite direct in their communication style.

At the other extreme, others speak slowly and deliberately, and pause between words. They tend to be less direct, often beating around the bush and taking a while to make a point or come to the heart of an issue.

One style is not better than the other, they're just different, but being aware of how others communicate when you meet them for the first time will give you great insight.

Another way of looking at different communication styles is whether someone is **open or closed**.

We've all met the person who gives us their life story in the first five minutes. In fact, they can often be quite charming people and the life of the party. Within minutes of meeting them, you'll already know a lot about them.

Others are more self-contained. Talking to them is sometimes like pulling teeth, it's hard to get to the bottom of who they are — and they play their cards very close to their chests.

People who are open tend to be relationship and people oriented, while those at the other end of the scale, self-contained people, tend to be task oriented. They prefer to focus on tasks, rather than other people.

While some people are squarely one type or another, most people sit somewhere on a scale, but most of us will have a dominant tendency towards being task or people focused.

Now let's overlay these two axes, these two ways of looking at behaviour, which gives you four quadrants:

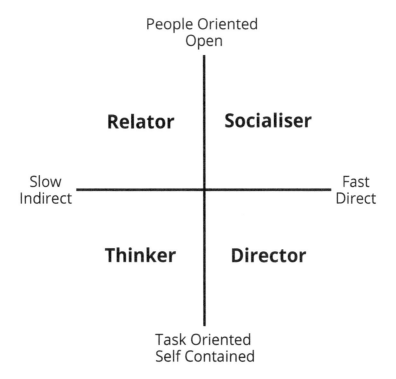

Those in the fast, open relationship quadrant are called **Socialisers**. They are people oriented, direct and very comfortable in company. Does this remind you of anyone in your life?

In the bottom right hand quadrant are fast-paced, direct task-based people that we call **Directors**. They like to get the job done. I bet you know some people like that, as well.

Across to the other side you have the slower-paced indirect, task-oriented people that we call **Thinkers**. These people take their time and analyse, analyse, analyse.

In the last quadrant you have slower-paced people who are not task oriented, but for whom relationships are more important — we call them the **Relators**.

As you can see, I've broken people down into four groups based on observable behaviours. Is this a people person, or is this a self-contained person? Are they fast or slow paced?

In fact, I ask myself these two questions when I meet people with whom I'm going to enter a negotiation or people whom I need to influence, because if I can get some indication of what type of person they are, I'm more likely to be able to influence them by being more like them.

Now let me be clear... some people will be at the extremes of these examples and others will fall somewhere along the spectrum. What I'm trying to do here is determine people's *predominant* style, but it is a fact that we behave differently in different situations and most of us don't fall nicely into just one category, we straddle across a couple.

But remember, this is all about building rapport, because people like people who are like them.

Now that you're starting to understand that we all express ourselves differently verbally and non-verbally, it's important to understand more about these differences so you can connect better with those you're planning to negotiate with, or sell to, or influence.

Recognising the different types of behavioural style

While this may not be the sort of information you expected in book on negotiation, please bear with me because even though the information you're learning is what has helped me become a great persuader, it's not the type of information most salespeople or negotiators ever learn about. This will put you ahead of the pack.

But first it will be critical for you to understand your own predominant personality style as probably 75% of the world will perceive things differently you, and your style will affect the way you communicate with others. Then to become a Power Negotiator you'll need to understand the characteristics of the other styles so you can relate better to them.

I want to go into quite some detail to help you recognise people's predominant behavioural styles, so let's get on with it.

SOCIALISERS

Socialisers are fast paced, open and people oriented. They love dealing with people, socialising, looking good, creative activities, being the centre of attention, and gaining recognition and approval from others.

Socialisers dislike dealing with details, working at a slow pace or boring activities. They tend to make decisions based on what other people are doing and are driven by social proof and social media.

You will find socialisers tending towards careers which involve creative activities, advertising, public relations, entertainment and hospitality but are particularly good at sales and marketing.

Stereotypical socialisers would include the late Robyn Williams, Jerry Seinfeld or Jim Carey.

DIRECTORS

In the lower right-hand corner of our quadrant are the fast paced, direct people who tend to be more self-contained and task oriented. Is this model we call them directors, and not surprisingly, this is what they like to do.

Directors like being in charge. They like power and leading, a fast pace, high achievement, success and money and looking good. Directors love building businesses and anything prestige.

Directors dislike unnecessary socialising, a slow pace, what they consider 'boring' or 'dumb' people, unnecessary detail and in particular they don't like being told what to do (and I know this well, being a director!).

They process data quickly and draw conclusions from it and take action, often recognising that they don't have all the information yet, but they take action anyway, knowing they'll find out the rest along the way.

You will often find directors running their own businesses or larger organisations or in senior management, showing high ticket items, building empires or anything BIG.

Stereotypical directors include Donald Trump, Steve Jobs, Bill Gates, Richard Branson and Rupert Murdoch. By the way… this is my predominant style, but now that I've learned the power of these concepts I can adapt my style to suit those I'm negotiating with.

THINKERS

In the lower left-hand corner of my quadrant are the Thinkers — those slow paced, task-oriented people who tend to… believe it or not… 'Think'.

Thinkers tend to be thorough, slow-paced, detailed oriented and enjoy technical or practical things including science. In general Thinkers dislike fast paced, flashy people and socialising.

Before making decisions, thinkers will listen carefully, ask questions and slowly absorb all the details. They process information methodically, rationally and logically. They work on facts and often double check the facts before reaching a conclusion. Thinkers don't jump to conclusions like directors do, they will do all the necessary research before making a decision.

You'll find thinkers choose career paths in accounting, engineering, science, IT and they make good solicitors (but not barristers who need to be more outgoing and people oriented enabling them to strut around in court).

Good examples of well-known thinkers are Albert Einstein and Stephen Hawkins.

This leaves us with the last personality style, in the top right-hand corner there are the slower paced relationship-oriented people we call the…

RELATORS

Relators like a relatively slow pace and being people oriented they love helping or counselling people.

Relators dislike fast paced or pushing people. They will make decisions based on the energy of others and other people's reactions more than based on facts.

You will find Relators in caring professions including teachers, particular kindergarten teachers, in medical professions and psychologists and in the human resources industries.

Good examples of relators include Lady Diana, Mother Teresa and Nelson Mandela.

Once again, there is no right or wrong style. There's no personality or behavioural style that is better than the others, and while many of us clearly fall into one of these four quadrants, at times, under different circumstances, we will behave differently.

In general, we all have a predominant behavioural style, and we have a style that we're definitely not, and then we tend to have a little bit of the other styles blended in.

But there's more...

There are other clues you can use to help determine a person's behavioural style because, not surprisingly, they have certain preferences in common. These not only relate to the jobs they do and the things they like, but also to the clothes they wear, the cars they drive, what motivates them and how best to influence them when you're planning to negotiate with them or sell to them.

WHAT DO THEY WEAR?

Socialisers tend to wear fashionable, colourful, trendy and sometimes even flamboyant clothes. They like wearing clothes that look expensive.

Directors dress for power in dark suits, red ties or maybe a scarf, and tend to wear expensive clothes.

Thinkers like to wear practical, inexpensive clothes. At seminars I get quite a laugh when I say thinkers like to shop at Kmart to buy clothes that others would describe as 'daggy', however thinkers see them as practical.

Relators often will wear loose, comfortable clothes, often neutral or beige colours because this won't offend anybody.

WHAT DO THEY DRIVE?

Socialisers like flashy cars — often red, sporty, fast looking cars.

Directors drive expensive cars that project power, often BMWs or Mercedes. They are often in dark power colours like black.

Thinkers tend to drive cheap, practical, often white compact cars. Unlike directors and Socialisers who like change, thinkers will often drive the same car for many years.

Relators favour conservative cars (that won't offend anyone) — a beige Volvo or people mover would be pretty typical.

WHAT DO THEY DO IN THEIR SPARE TIME?

Socialisers like to… socialise. They like to party and make new friends. You'll find them on social media and using the latest apps.

Directors have little spare time, preferring to work. They're good at competitive sport because they like to win, and they enjoy building relationships and networks especially if this helps their business.

Thinkers like to collect things, do research, play computer games and build small models etc.

Relators enjoying family and community activities or volunteer work and many are out to 'save the planet'.

STRENGTHS AND WEAKNESSES:

Socialisers tend to be fun to be with and are generally enthusiastic, highly motivated and can be persuasive. However, they tend to be poor with detail, often disorganised and not good at taking care of loose ends. Time management is not one of their strengths and they often have many projects on the go, because they're excited about doing more things, but often projects get left uncompleted as they lose interest and move onto the next shiny toy.

Directors strengths are that they get the job done. They are high achievers, move fast and are usually strong leaders. If you asked a director what his weaknesses were, they would boldly tell you they have no weaknesses. But like everyone, they have a downside, including the fact that their style often annoys or offends others as they are fast paced, impatient and don't suffer fools. Many would call them workaholics.

Thinkers strengths include their thoroughness, reliability and attention to detail. However, on the flipside, they can be inflexible, slow and frustrate people as they get bogged down in detail, stuck in 'analysis paralysis', meaning they tend not to make decisions. I 'think' this is in part this is because they love the process much more than achieving final result.

Relators strengths are that they are caring, very good with people and building and maintaining relationships. They are good listeners and as they genuinely caring people, you often find them on committees or community support organisations. The downside of this however is that they sometimes care 'too much' and are too easily swayed by others' point of view, not wanting to offend people and this can be seen as a weakness. Relators do not make strong leaders as they don't like to confront people.

What's your style?

By now you should've started to work out your predominant style. Are you fast paced or slow? Are you people oriented or task oriented?

Remember… we all have a secondary style and the style you exhibit will vary depending upon your environment.
While I'm a strong director style, imagine how far that would

get me at home with my wife and my children. I behave differently and more caringly with them, and I have learned the power of adapting my style to interact differently with my team and clients. This has made things easier for me and for them and life is much more fun that way.

How to negotiate with the different personality styles

I hope you're starting to understand that these different styles have a different way in which they see the world. They take in information differently, they express themselves differently, they think differently, they have different factors that motivate them or irritate them, and this means they negotiate differently.

That's why to successfully negotiate with or persuade or influence others, you have to understand their predominance style.

Think about it…

What would happen if you were a Socialiser trying to negotiate with a Thinker? You'd probably want to have some fun, discuss things over a coffee, then move on fast to the next deal. On the other hand, the Thinker would want to make sure they were taking all the details into account and they would not be ready to move on until they 'covered all their bases'.

The Thinker would probably see you as a fast, high pressured, possibly flashy salesperson; while you'd probably consider them slow and irritating.

Can you see how this could lead to either a poor negotiating outcome or worse still to a degree of conflict?

It's much the same if a Director was attempting to negotiate with the Relator. The Director wants to get to the bottom line quickly, get the deal done and make a profit. On the other hand, the Relator would want to move slowly and examine the consequences of the deal. They would most likely see the Director as abrupt and arrogant, while the Director could well see the Relator as unrealistically idealistic and out of touch with the 'real world'.

I hope you can now see how each of these behavioural styles would come into the same situation from a different perspective. And the styles likely to clash the most are Directors and Relators (who are the opposite corners of the diagram above) and Thinkers and Socialisers.

But there is a way to negotiate with other behavioural styles

Put simply… the answer is you need to be able to adapt your behaviour and be flexible.

This starts with an understanding your own behavioural style, how you communicate and how you like to negotiate. And just as importantly you need to understand where the other party fits in, where they are coming from, their predominant way of communicating, what motivates them and what irritates them.

Interestingly this all gets back to developing rapport, maximising sameness and minimising differences.

To help you understand how this would work in a negotiating situation, let's look at some further aspects of each style so you can take these into consideration when negotiating with them.

Just to make things clear… using this information to make you more persuasive is not being devious, it's just understanding the science of human behaviour to help even the odds in your favour. Let's delve deeper and understand more about each of these four styles so you can 'get into the head' of those you want to influence.

SOCIALISERS

Fears: loss of face (remember it's important for to them to look good), rejection, boredom.
Under tension: they can become sarcastic and attack.
What they seek: recognition.
Need to know: how what you're offering will enhance their image or status. Who else has bought this, or used your services and benefited? They like social proof.
Gain security through: flexibility — they like lots of options to choose from.
What motivates them: a fun environment, recognition, money and the opportunity to look good.
To support them: they like to be heard, so listen to them.
Irritated by: completing paperwork (okay today much of it

is done on a computer, but they don't like routine), anything boring, thinkers.

They like you to be: stimulating, interesting and fast paced.

They want to be: admired. They love having egos stroked and they love compliments.

Measure their personal worth: by their friendships and relationships and by acknowledgement of their achievements by others.

They make decisions: very quickly but watch out, they can change their minds just as quickly, so negotiate with them to conclude the deal in writing quickly.

DIRECTORS

Fears: failure and loss of control — their stress levels will go up if they're feeling out of control.

Under tension: they will become assertive and dictatorial and can become quite arrogant.

What they seek: productivity, return on investment and bottom line results.

Need to know: they only want bullet points, but need to know what your proposal will do for them, particularly what it will cost them return of it for their money.

Gain security: when they are in control.

What motivates them: give them responsibility, a fast-paced environment, competition and a chance to excel and they will. They like big rewards, ego rewards, no limitations and the chance to look good.

To support them: show them how you can help them achieve their goals.

Irritated by: inefficiency, time wasters, unreliable people, broken agreements, slow people, bureaucracy, authority, perceived weakness, all other styles (they just can't see why others don't think like them).

They achieve acceptance: through leadership, being competitive and when winning.

They like you to be: brief and to the point.

They want to be: in charge, so in negotiations you must make them feel this if they are in control even if they're not.

Measure their personal worth: by their status and wealth.

They make decisions: quickly and change them slowly.

THINKERS

Fears: making mistakes. They worry about what other people would think of them if they made a wrong decision.

Under tension: they will become withdrawn.

What they seek: accuracy in their own work, precision and accuracy in other people. To them the process is more important than the outcome.

Need to know: lots of details. When negotiating with Thinkers give them facts and logical reasons to make a decision. The challenge is not to give too many facts so that they get stuck in analysis paralysis.

Gain security through: preparation and research.

What motivates them: Making improvements, systems and processes, technical aspects.

To support them: let them take their time, compliment the level of detail they are pursuing, be patient and show them why choosing your solution will stop them making a mistake (the thing I fear the most).

Irritated by: inaccuracy, time constraints, surprises (such as new information brought to the table while you're trying to make up their mind), generalisations and the big picture (given them details), fast paced people including Socialisers.

They pride themselves: in their correctness and a thoroughness.

They like you to be: precise.

They want to be: correct, cannot make any mistakes.

Measure their personal worth: by the precision of their work, their thoroughness.

They make decisions: very slowly and deliberately.

RELATORS

Fears: confrontation and offending others. They may not even say what's on their minds if they fear it will offend others.

Under tension: they will concede and give in.

What they seek: to be understood.

Need to know: how the proposal will affect them and those they care about — sometimes how it will affect larger groups like their community, country or the world — they hate globalisation.

Gain security: through close relationships.

What motivates them: looking after people, relationships, customer service, developing people, community.

To support them: ask them questions, listen carefully and seek to understand the feelings behind their words.

Irritated by: pushy, fast paced or insensitive people, insincerity and time pressures.

They achieve acceptance by: loyalty and the quality of their relationships.

They like you to be: personable. They will want to get to know you, that you are genuine and that you care about them and people in general.

They want to be: liked and approved of.

Measure their personal worth: by the quality and depth of their relationships.

They make decisions: after careful consideration.

To negotiate with the different personality styles

Each style has strengths and weaknesses in how they negotiate, so let's look at them:

THE SOCIALISER

They tend to be assertive, reactive, impulsive and make decisions spontaneously, but they change their minds quickly. They are emotionally expressive, sometimes dramatic and place more importance on relationships than tasks. They have strong persuasive skills and are talkative and gregarious. But one of their negotiating weaknesses is that they rely on their ability to get you excited about what they're suggesting believing that if you get excited enough, you'll go for it.

To negotiate with Socialisers, first seek out their opinions and achieve mutual understanding — build rapport with them. If possible, centre your discussion around people, as well as the facts. And as they are flighty, keep summarising and work out specifics on points of agreement. They love short, fast moving stories about people's experiences and remember to discuss the future, as well as the present.

Watch out for their impulse agreements as they're likely to change their minds so when you've come a final agreement make sure to document it. It also helps to get them to verbalise the summary of the agreed discussion points at the end, to ensure that they are still on the same page and solidify their buy-in.

THE DIRECTOR

In negotiations the Director is out to win — none of this win/win stuff for them. They may even think that unless the other person loses, or gives concessions, they can't call the negotiation a real win.

They tend to be assertive, decisive and determined and control their emotions. Remember they like to be in control, they're often inflexible, impatient and in a hurry and are poor listeners.

To negotiate with Directors, give them a sense of control.

Plan to ask questions about and discuss specifics, actions and results. Directors will respect you more if you are assertive, so use facts and logic and when necessary, disagree with facts rather than opinions. Keep the negotiation business-like, efficient and to the point.

While the more people-oriented styles love personal guarantees and testimonials, directors look to the bottom line and want to see facts and options.

THE THINKER

Thinkers are usually analytical and detached, rigid and inflexible in their negotiations. They prefer precise, orderly and business-like negotiations and are motivated by logic and facts.

They're slow in making decisions — remember they hate making mistakes; and they distrust pushy salespeople. They like detail and things in writing but are sometimes too inflexible and too detached and set in their ways to be able to create a win/win result easily.

To negotiate with Thinkers, stick to specifics, as their decisions are based on facts and logic as they try and avoid risk. It's usually worth telling them what your product or service won't do or achieve — they will respect you for it and they will have probably spotted the deficiencies anyway.

Slow down the negotiations, discuss reasons and ask 'why' questions and give them enough information to make a decision, but not so much that they get stuck in analysis paralysis.

It's important to move thinkers from a 'thinking' space to more of a feeling space if you can — that will help them make decisions. Remember, Thinkers have their emotional/feeling side too, so it helps to tap into this especially when the negotiations get too bogged down in the nitty-gritty.

THE RELATOR

In negotiations, Relators are forever seeking to be understood and they want to reach agreement as their objective is often not so much to win as to make sure everybody is happy.

A major fault of Relators is that they arc too easily swayed by other people's point of view. They tend to get taken advantage of in the negotiating situation, because they falsely believe that if they give enough concessions and the other people will do the same. Of course, this doesn't always happen.

To negotiate with Relators, find out about their personal interests and their family. Don't rush or seem pushy, instead take time to be agreeable and seek common ground. Be patient and avoid going for what looks like an easy pushover and don't take advantage of their good nature.

They like certainty so use personal assurances and specific guarantees and avoid options and probabilities. Demonstrate low risk solutions to them.

I hope you're starting to understand that to become a power negotiator, you're going to have to learn more that some fancy lines or how to handle objections. You're going to have to understand how your prospect thinks, feels, communicates and what they want because your success will depend on you treating people how they want to be treated.

Clearly this is different to the Golden Rule 'treat others as **you want** to be treated' because if you do, misunderstandings are inevitable. You're assuming your counterpart values the same things you do. They don't!

So you'll need to get to understand them by building rapport. Which is what I'm going to explain in more detail in the next chapter.

THE ART OF BUILDING RAPPORT – MIRRORING AND MATCHING

■ ■ ■

You're probably aware that nonverbal cues play a huge role in communicating how we think or feel. Even those with a very good poker face, give away what they think through how they stand, sit, gesticulate or address the other person.

Once upon a time, people didn't give that much thought to nonverbal communication, or body language as it has become known. They presumed that the dominant form of communication was verbal. And that makes sense, doesn't it? You communicate through what you say, the information you relay.

Then, in 1967, the *Journal of Consulting Psychology* published a study that turned everything on its head. The study involved subjects listening to nine recorded words, three conveying like (honey, dear and thanks), three conveying neutrality (maybe, really and oh) and three conveying dislike (don't, brute and terrible).

The words were spoken with different tonalities and subjects were asked to guess the emotions behind the words. The result was that tone and emotion carried more meaning than the individual words themselves.

A second study re-affirmed their findings. Using another set of nine words with different emotions, they found a person's response to each word was dependent on the tone of the voice rather than the literal meaning of the word or phrase.

These studies led researchers to claim that the interpretation of a message is 7%based on the words you say, 38% comes from the tone of your voice vocal and 55% from the speaker's body language and face. This means that 93% of communication is 'nonverbal' in nature.

What this means for you

This has huge implications for you as a negotiator. If you're only just becoming aware of body language, then the truth is you've been communicating messages to people without realising it.

Once you are aware of how body language works you can then adjust yours to send the right message. You can learn how to stand, greet and interact with people, while sending the right verbal cues.

Crucially, you'll also be able to read other people and know when they're genuinely interested in a deal, and how much power they have in the negotiation setting.

Let me explain it another way…

Have you seen those photos on Facebook where an owner ends up looking like their pet? Well I'm not sure if that's true but maybe you've noticed that when best friends get together, they tend to act and even sound alike?

Now that's no coincidence. Behavioural research show that mirroring and matching —copying other people's body language, mannerisms and repeating their words — establishes rapport and helps build trust.

Charismatic influencers do this instinctively but building rapport by mirroring and matching can be learned and it's a skill I was taught when I studied Neuro-linguistic Programming (NLP), an interpersonal communication model created by Richard Bandler and John Grinder in the 1970s.

I believe I first became aware of NLP when well-known life coach Tony Robbins convinced me to walk over hot coals in his famous fire walk on the first night of his three-day powerful workshop. Now I just went along to his seminar to see others do that — after all I'm not that silly or susceptible am I? But Tony's powerful language patterns worked on me.

I was so impressed that I studied NLP for a number of years, including attending a number of Tony Robbins bootcamps, as well as courses from a number of local NLP trainers, including Chris Howard, and it has improved relationships in every aspect of my life.

Along the way I learned that all the persuasive public speakers applied NLP techniques as did influencers in all walks of life. And boy is it prevalent in advertising.

One of the first lessons I learned in NLP was the importance of building rapport, especially as the first step in any serious negotiation or any time you want to influence or persuade someone. Rapport increases the sameness between you and the other person and minimising the differences.

Most people find it easy to relate to (build rapport with) people who are like themselves but find it hard to build rapport with people who are different. Meaning if you're in the world of sales or persuasion, this obviously limits your possibilities.

Imagine if I asked you to go to a bar or a networking function and build rapport with someone you'd never met before. How would you go about doing this? You'd probably first start by asking them a lot of questions. But that won't necessarily create rapport — how often have you started this type of conversation, but it led to nothing?

That's because questions alone don't build rapport. Rapport is created by a feeling of commonality.

The problem is that most salespeople or negotiators try to create commonality by using words, but research shows us that only around 7% of our communication is generated by words, so using words alone means you're leaving out 93% of your potential to communicate.

When studying NLP I learned the techniques of **matching** and **mirroring** which are based on the idea that people feel most comfortable around those who are like them — they feel that their point of view is understood. The more someone believes you are like them, the easier to develop trust and rapport at the unconscious level.

Mirroring refers to the simultaneous 'copying' of the behaviour of another person, as if reflecting their movements back to them. When done with respect and discretion, mirroring creates a positive feeling and responsiveness in you and the other person.

Matching, on the other hand, is much the same but has a little 'time lag'. For example, if a seated client uncrosses his legs and leans slightly inward while speaking, you should wait for a few seconds and then discretely adopt the same posture.

These techniques were based on the teachings of Milton H. Erickson, a psychiatrist who understood that we have a conscious and a subconscious mind and the subconscious mind is much more powerful. He realised that if he could influence the subconscious mind, he could help his patients. Often in just one session of therapy.

Erickson recognised that when people were in rapport with each other they became more like each other in a variety of ways. In his words — they *mirrored* each other. We all mirror people we are close to or admire it's something we do naturally and are not aware of.

Again, this is based on the fact that people like people who are like themselves or how they would like to be. And, in general, people don't like people who are not like them.

Let's do a little test. Think of someone you like a lot and now ask yourself — are they like you or like someone you'd like to be?

Now think of someone you don't like. You'll probably find they are *not* like you or like someone you'd like to be?

So how can you use this knowledge to become a more powerful persuader?

As I said, you've been mirroring certain people all your life — you've been mirroring people who you've been in rapport with and you've done so subconsciously.

The fact is that when we meet others for the first time, we tend to quickly assess whether they are positive or negative towards us. This probably goes back to our cave man days when we did this for survival reasons. Mirroring is also left over from a primitive method of learning which involved imitation.

We do this by scanning the other person's body to see if they move or gesture in the same way as we do. If they're mirroring us.

At the same time, we're mirroring others all the time as a way of bonding, being accepted and creating rapport. That's why members of bike gangs all ride the same bikes, wear the same leather jackets and wear similar helmets. Sure that's an extreme example, but do you see what I mean?

Mirroring makes others feel at ease and sends the non-verbal clue 'Hey look at me. I'm the same as you. I share similar thoughts and attitudes'.

Now that you're starting to understand the importance of this you should consciously start mirroring people you want to build rapport with. That's what I did it when I was first taught these techniques well over 20 years ago. Having done this for years now, today mirroring and matching others is second nature to me.

I do it unconsciously and it helps me build rapport quickly every time I see a potential new client, or whenever I enter into a negotiation or even when I speak on stage in front of hundreds of people or online to thousands of people (even though the way I do this is very different from how I do it one-on-one).

I remember when I was first taught these concepts I was told that if I wanted to build rapport quickly I should sit like the other party would sit, and talk at a similar pace to the other person and breath at a similar pace to them. In other words, copy their unconscious elements of communication.

But that's not what most people do. They wait to mirror their counterpart *after* they've asked lots of questions and shared lots of words. They wait until they have had enough words in common and only then do they try and put their body, posture and voice in common. But as you now know, your words only make up 7% of your communication.

As I explained, we judge other people in a matter of seconds by their style. Have you ever run into someone who has grated on you right from the start? Maybe it was the tone of their voice that drove you up the wall.

So imagine you're keen to build rapport with someone you just met what could you do?

If you were dealing with them over the phone you could really only match and mirror a few things such as their...

Tone / Inflection Volume:

Mirroring aspects of someone (their tone, rate, volume, etc.) is most effective when done subtly. Your 'mirrored' voice should never be radically different from your own, but if the other party talks quietly and you have a loud voice, can you imagine how they could feel overwhelmed?

You'd also mirror their *pace* — if they talked slowly and you talked at a fast pace how connected do you think they'd feel? Do you think they'd trust you? Matching the *pace* of their speech creates a sense of alignment and allows you to more easily match their energy level. You'll often find that people who live in our big cities speak much more quickly than those form regional locations.

Words:

You'd also mirror the *key words* the other person said. Imagine you sold real estate and a potential client comes in saying they want a home with a *fantastic* view of the bay. Now it so happens you have such a home for sale, but you'd be shooting yourself in the foot if you told them you've got a home with *magnificent* water views. Those words may mean the same to you, but probably not to your prospect — they want *fantastic* bay views, NOT a *magnificent* home with views of the water.

A great way of mirroring words is *repeating the last few words* (or the critical few words) that someone says to you.

For example, if someone comes up to you and says: 'Have you got a few minutes to talk?' you would say: 'A few minutes to talk?' Or if they say, 'I'm looking to buy a new home', you'd say, 'Buy a new home?'

And you'd repeat this technique a few times during the conversation because it's one of the quickest ways to establish rapport as it keeps the other party talking and they eventually feel safe enough to reveal themselves.

Sensory Predicates:

This is really the next level up in mirroring words because you'll understand why your counterpart is using certain words.

You see… most of us tend to favour one of four types of sensory-based systems that help us understand our world and experiences. We tend to be either:

- Visual
- Auditory
- Kinaesthetic/Feeling
- Auditory-Digital

While most of us use all four sensory systems in our vocabulary, we tend to favour one in particular when we choose words to describe our experiences. So it's very helpful to pick up on key words that reveal a person's underlying favoured system, so that you can repeat those or similar words to build rapport and meaningful connections.

For example:

- *Visual Predicates* include words and phrases such as: see, look, view, foggy, clear, bright, reveal, focused, short-sighted, paint a picture, an eyeful, picture this, hazy, etc.
- *Auditory Predicates* include terms and phrases such as: sound, hear, tell, listen, resonate, clear as a bell, loud-and-clear, tune in/out, on another note, give me your ear, etc.
- *Kinaesthetic/Feeling Predicates* include words and phrases such as: touch, feel, grasp, fuzzy, hard, concrete, sharp as a tack, solid, unfeeling, heated debate, get in touch with, make contact, hand-in-hand, etc.
- *Auditory Digital Predicates include* words and phrases such as: think, know, learn, process, decide, consider, understand, experience, motivate, learn, figure it out, make sense of, pay attention to, word-for-word, conceive, etc.

People integrate these predicates into their language, and if you detect them you can incorporate similar words into your dialogue. This results in a stronger feeling of connection because you're 'talking the same language'. You're communicating in a way that is familiar and comfortable for the other party so they're more likely to trust you.

For example, if a client says to me, 'I like the look of the contract. The bottom-line is clear and your suggested plan is focused', I would reply with something like, 'I'm glad that I was able to paint a clear picture of the path ahead; let's see how we can work together toward a common vision for your future.'

See what I did? My client's underlying system of communication was overwhelmingly visual, and I responded accordingly. By the way, my preferred style of communication is auditory, but by speaking their language I built trust.

I've found this technique a major influencer in building rapport, but surprisingly most negotiators never use it.

Now let's move it up a notch

Of course, when dealing with people face to face you can really take your matching and mirroring to the next level by observing their...

Posture

I remember learning how body language often reflects our feelings and attitudes. This means that when you mirror and match a person's body posture, you actually begin to understand more about them.

Is your client sitting, standing, relaxing or slouching? Are her legs or arms crossed? Is he leaning in any particular direction? Are her feet together or apart? Are they holding anything in their hands, such as a pen or cup of coffee?

If the other party crosses their legs or places their hands on a table, wait for 4–5 seconds then match that in the same way. The same applies to shifting to another position, hand placement, etc. Observe how they move. If they move quickly and you move slowly, your patterns are out of sync. Speed yourself up just a bit or slow down until you're both comfortable with one another.

Gestures

People often use gestures along with posture to give insight on how they categorise their experiences.

Observe the other party and see if they gesture with their hands in a particular way, or with a nod or tilt of their head? Are their hand gestures exaggerated and expansive, or protective and restrictive? Discreetly mirror the gestures of the person you're listening to — if they lean their head to the left, wait a few seconds and lean to the right (which is their left).

Energy Level

Some people are naturally relaxed while others are gregarious.

NLP teaches us to match the other party's energy level to build rapport. An effective way to do this is to mirror their breathing rate. I've found this is one of the most difficult aspects to match as it requires you to closely observe the rise and fall of the other party's chest and shoulders, among other cues, while simultaneously maintaining consistent eye contact and engaging in deep listening — it could be pretty embarrassing if it looked like you were staring at their chest. However, once mastered, it's very effective.

Proximity

Every person likes a certain amount of space around that so they can feel comfortable.

Some people stand too far away, and others stand too close. Make sure you have a good sense of what a healthy distance feels like, so you can put others at ease and feel relaxed as well.

I've found that people who live in big cities need a smaller comfort zone around them. While people from the country tend to like more space around them.

Have you ever had someone come right up to you and you've felt uncomfortable — the expression we use is 'in your face', isn't it? But if you pull back you've broken rapport as that's what they need to feel good.

The best way to pick someone's comfort zone is to use your sensory acuity to assess their level of comfort as you move closer to the other party. How are they breathing? This increases if they get tense. What are their facial expressions? Are they moving back or turning sideways?

Eye contact

People as a rule, look away when they speak and hold eye contact for longer when they're listening.

If someone looks away when you look at them and fails to hold eye contact then this may be a sign they're trying to hide what they really feel.

The opposite is true, too: maintaining eye contact is a sign that someone is engaged with what you are saying.

If a person's eyes are dilated then this is a good sign they like you and are more likely to do business with you.

Touch

For certain people you can build more rapport with the right touch than any other technique. But done incorrectly or to the wrong people it instantly creates a barrier rather than a closeness.

A light touch on the arm, expertly delivered at the right time and place, can close a deal. But it helps if you have some rapport with the person and a good working relationship.

However, be careful of touching people who may not be comfortable with it. People have very different comfort levels when it comes to touch so tread carefully and rarely take the initiative. If someone else is a toucher, then use this to your advantage by copying their behaviour.

Shake on it

Often in business you'll greet someone by shaking hands — when you do this note the type of handshake they have. Are they a squeezer or do they have a limp fish handshake? If you have a firm handshake but the other party doesn't, don't squeeze their hand — be like them and reciprocate with a limp handshake.

I've found a handshake offers many insights into a person's personality and even their level of confidence. One study conducted by the University of Alabama found that many people could predict what kind of personality the person they shook hands with had. And guess what? Those offering firm and confident handshakes were considered to be more outgoing and positive people.

Also, notice how the other party touches their assistant if they have one. If they pat them on the shoulder three times saying, 'Thanks Bob, you've done a great job', you'll rapidly build rapport if there is an appropriate occasion for you to pet him three times on the should and say, 'Thank you John.'

Get up

This is a tip that may sound a little old fashioned, but I think it's a good one. The number one way to convey respect and confidence is to stand when the person — your client, the other party, the seller — walks in the room, whether they are male or female.

Now you don't have to do it every time they leave and re-enter the room — this isn't a 19th century novel — but if you are waiting for them in a room and they enter to meet with you, then stand and shake their hand.

Even if you've met with them before or know them pretty well, try to refrain from offering a meek 'hey' from the comfort of your chair.

People notice little things like that these days because we're so rushed and we've forgotten our manners along the way. Try it and you'll see what I mean.

Calm things down

There will come times when you're negotiating that things get a little tense. Perhaps you have reached an impasse and the other party is getting a little hot under the collar (you won't be because as an expert negotiator you realise that this is not productive).

You can use your tone and your language to calm things down, but you can also use your nonverbal communication too.

When things get tense focus on calming your body and maybe even take a deep breath. This will enable your body to relax which the other person will pick up on. Keep your body open and facing towards them and resist the urge to slap the table, cross your arms or roll your eyes.

You want to be as calm in heated situations as you are in less-demanding ones.

Time to try these techniques

Mirroring someone's body language makes them feel accepted and creates rapport and it's a phenomenon that occurs naturally between friends and people of equal status.

If you're looking to influence or persuade someone, mirroring their body language and speech patterns is one of the most powerful techniques for quickly establishing rapport. Before long they'll start to feel there is something about you they like. You'll be easy to be with because they see something of themselves reflected in you.

However, do use common sense and discretion. Don't outright mimic a person's every move — that's counterproductive and insincere. If your counterpart becomes aware that you're actively using specific techniques to create rapport with them, there's a good chance that their state of trust and receptivity will be irrevocably eroded.

And of course, don't mirror and match negative body language.

We automatically mirror and match people with whom we feel comfortable. When we practice these techniques with intention and respect, we can enhance our communication with others and achieve greater levels of success in our personal and professional relationships.

Why not try these ideas out on a few people with whom you'd like to build a more meaningful relationship. See if they work as well for you as they have for me.

Ways to get people to like you in the first 10 seconds they meet you

Here's a simple way to start using the principles I've just taught you to get people to like you when you first meet them so that you can more easily build rapport and influence them.

1. *Adjust your attitude* — adjust your attitude to take get rid of any negative feelings or pre supposed prejudices you bring to the conversation. We sometimes have inbuilt biases and discriminations, already assuming things about your prospects

2. *Smile*

3. *Look people in the eyes*

4. *Raise your eyebrows* — this shows that you're curious and engaged

5. *Shake hands* — this makes a connection — remember how I've already mentioned this?

6. *Lean in* towards the other person

7. *Use Open body language (vs Closed)* — for example, use welcoming gesture as opposed to having your arms crossed, keep your palms open rather having clenched fists.

Use these seven little tricks correctly and you could do to tip the needle towards likability pretty quickly.

Finally, trust your gut

Sometimes you get a feeling that someone is ready to sign a deal. It's not necessarily what they're saying or how they're behaving, it's more of a gut instinct. This is very powerful and should be listened to because these types of instincts are what separates great negotiators from brilliant ones.

The truly brilliant negotiator puts all of the theory into play and then they fall back on instinct: reading the subtle signs of the other person to know when to push the deal, back off or change tack.

This kind of instinct can be honed, too, through years of practice and soon, like the experienced negotiators, you know when to play your hand and when to hold and much of it won't require too much active thinking, it will simply feel natural to you.

In the next chapter, I'll show you more ways of understanding what's going on in the minds of those you want to influence.

HOW TO GET INSIDE THE HEAD OF YOUR PROSPECTS

■ ■ ■

While this particular chapter is mainly aimed at people involved in sales, as I've already mentioned we are all in sales, so don't discard the importance of this information even if your job description doesn't include sales.

Similarly, even if you heard some of these concepts before, please take the time to read them again and see how well you're implementing the information you already know.

Let's begin with one of the lessons I learned from my early mentors in marketing, the late Dan Kennedy, who taught me the importance of getting inside of the head of my potential customers or clients. And this principal is clearly just as applicable if you are involved in negotiation.

You see... you can't conduct a successful sale or a powerful negotiation until you know what the other party really wants or desires.

In a sale situation most salespeople believe they should sell what the prospect needs. While that may be a noble cause, the fact is most people buy what they *want*, not what they *need*. They buy what they desire and then justify their emotional purchase with logic trying to justify it to themselves as a need.

A few years ago I bought an expensive Bentley sports car. It's something I really wanted, in fact it was the dream car I've wanted for years, but I live two minutes from work and drive less than 5,000km a year. I absolutely did not *need* a new Bentley. A less expensive car would have been just as functional — in fact I sold a perfectly good two-year-old Jaguar to buy my Bentley.

But I bought with my emotions and then justified the purchase to myself by saying that I was able to write off the car as a tax deduction in my business and that I was able to lease the car at a very low interest rate and this would become a further tax deduction.

Yes... I bought emotionally and justified my decision logically.

OK… maybe you haven't bought such an expensive car but, like me, you're likely to have bought the latest smartphone even though yours was only one or two years old. And you probably bought it emotionally because you wanted to keep up with your friends who bought one and then justified it by convincing yourself that you needed the better camera or more storage space for your photos.

So to become successful in sales, negotiation or influence you need to find out what your prospect wants. What they desire. What motivates them at a deeper level. Only then will you have the power to influence them. Only then will you be in a negotiating position to offer what perfectly matches what your prospect ardently desires. Only then will you be able to put together an offer that becomes almost irresistible.

Just to make things clear... in any decision-making process, the is an emotional and irrational element. So it's a terrible mistake to try and negotiate or persuade the other party's rational brain. That's because people usually make their decisions emotionally, and then rationalise that decision with the thinking half of their brain. When you understand this, you can focus on the emotional level of the negotiation. What need are you satisfying? What fears are you either tapping into or helping the other party avoid?

As you will learn in this chapter, to touch the other party's emotional brain you'll need to speak in the language of pleasure or pain, of desire or fear. When speaking to the rational brain it's important to understand that it's not actually driven by logic so much as the need to look good or to avoid embarrassment. In other words, our rational brain is very much driven by the emotions of vanity and insecurity.

How do you motivate someone to take action?

There are two main motivators for people to take action — inspiration and desperation. This is just another way of saying pleasure or pain.

Inspiration is tied in emotion and the longer term. It's creating something special, exploring what's possible. Studies show that inspiration is a motivator that produces positive feelings. When people feel inspired by something greater than themselves, they get motivated. Great leaders inspire you.

On the other hand, *desperation* is rooted in logic and is more short term, such as financial or health problems or stress. Even proving oneself to others, ego-involvement, gaining extrinsic rewards is a form of desperation.

The problem for most of us is that we're too comfortable. We struggle to step outside of that comfort zone and therefore never make much progress where we need it most.

As I see it, there are only two reasons people leave their comfort zone:

1. There is something inside they don't want.
2. There is something outside our comfort zone they want.

So to become a powerful persuader you'll need to find the motivation of those you're trying to influence. You'll need to find unmet needs and wants, find your prospects pain or their point of desperation. You'll need to make their dreams more real than their fears.

Success and growth comes from the discomfort of moving outside your comfort zone and eventually discomfort becomes comfortable as they recognise new patterns.

If you want to make a sale – create a gap

A good negotiator knows you can only get a person to act when there is a gap between their current situation and their desire — what they want their situation to be.

As a sales professional it is your job to define that gap for them and then clearly show your prospect how they can achieve it. In essence you're a *problem detective*. Your job is to find problems, needs or gaps for which your product or service is the ideal solution.

Let me explain this further using the ABC model of human behaviour and motivation.

The 'A' represents the antecedent event — a state of felt dissatisfaction. That is why, after all, the prospect is negotiating with you.

The 'B' is the product, service, idea or action that you're trying to persuade the person to buy because they're not happy with the status quo of 'A'.

And, you guessed it, the 'C' represents a state of intense satisfaction or relief: the answer to whatever problem or issue they were trying to change or solve.

As a negotiator, you need to identify the benefit of a certain course of action, and you do this by highlighting the gap between the current position and the other party's desired outcome. You should focus on the transformation that will occur — how much better a person will *feel* after they take a certain course of action. The reason they'll feel better is because their life will start to resemble the one they want in their mind, and that is a very potent negotiation tool.

To take this a step further, the size of the gap and the clarity of the solution you're proposing will usually determine how much a person is willing to pay for your service or product. They need to feel the gap is real and the transformation you can provide is significant enough to take action. If there's a big difference people will pay a lot to bridge the gap, while on the flip side, if the gap is small then they won't be keen to part with much.

That's why trying to sell on the basis of a low price is such a bad idea. Instead, try to focus on creating as wide a gap as possible so your prospect can see the value that you bring them by offering a bridge between 'A' and 'C'.

There is another way to look at human motivation using the ABC model, and I learned this approach from another one of my early sales mentors, motivational public speaker Brian Tracy.

He taught me that when negotiating, it is really important to understand what is going through the other person's mind when they're weighing up a certain course of action.

If you're in sales, if you're negotiating, you want people to act now rather than later, so being aware of human motivation can give you the edge.

Tracey has a slightly different ABC model.

His 'A' still stands for *antecedents* — the factors that lead up to (and influence) any course of action.

Tracey's 'B' stands for the *behaviour* that a person undertakes as a result of some impulse of decision.

And his 'C' stands for the *consequences* of that particular behaviour based on the antecedent that motivated the behaviour.

After studying and training salespeople for years, Tracy discovered that around 85% of a person's behaviour is motivated by what they anticipate happening in the future as a result of engaging in a particular behaviour, such as buying a product or service. In other words, people do what they do because they think of what's going to happen if they buy or sell a particular product or service or engage in any particular action.

In reality, since we're all emotional beings, we tend to buy what we buy based on how we imagine feeling as a result of owning and enjoying a particular product or service. The upshot of all this is, of course, that what you're actually selling is a feeling, because that is what people are anticipating and imagining when they buy something. Subconsciously they think about how they will feel once that decision has been made rather than the specifics of the goods they're purchasing.

I'll explain this a bit better in a moment when I discuss outcomes and transformation, so please bear with me.

Continuing with this train of thought...if your prospect imagines a happy feeling, a contented feeling, they will be motivated to act based on that emotion. They know that they have to part with money or time to achieve that feeling, as there usually is some sacrifice involved, but they're not fussed because they value that feeling over the financial sacrifice.

They also realise that they could use the same amount of money to buy something else but it would hold less value for them. This is all playing on their mind when they're weighing up the decision.

Remember customers always have three choices:
1. They can buy from you,
2. They can buy from someone else, or
3. They can do nothing at all.

As a sales professional, you have to show them that, all things considered, buying goods or services from you at this particular time is the best choice.

It took a graphic example, offered by Brian Tracy, that really brought this message home to me.

Imagine you went to a restaurant to have dinner and you look through the menu. You decide to order the dish that you think will give you the greatest satisfaction out of all the items on the menu. Now this doesn't mean that the other items on the menu are not as good tasting as the one you choose. It simply means that at that moment, rightly or wrongly, you feel that what you chose will give you the greatest satisfaction of all the options that are available to you.

If you think about it, this is really what you do when you shop at the supermarket or when you buy clothes anticipating how you will feel wearing a particular item of clothing as compared to the other items that are available at the same time and at the same price.

The fact is, you can't buy everything you want to buy. You simply don't have enough money, so you have to choose between the various options available and you choose on the basis of how you feel you will be afterwards.

Everything you do is done in anticipation of the emotion or feeling that you will experience once the decision has been made.

Understanding these A,B,C's will help you to see just how emotionally driven people are, and that it can change from moment to moment.

The best negotiators are those that can create a gap and then bridge it.

Let's look at this concept a little further…

Dave Dee, also a student of Dan Kennedy and one of my mentors who has taught me a lot about sales, explains that you can read your prospect's minds by asking yourself a number of questions. These are explained in his great book *Sales Stampede*.

1. What keeps your prospects awake at night?
Science shows us that people are motivated by a desire to avoid pain and a desire to gain pleasure. In fact, we are much more motivated to avoid pain than we are in gaining pleasure. So if you can determine what is keeping your prospect awake at night, what is worrying them, then you can create an offer that solves their specific problem.

Then by pushing their emotional hot buttons (remember we buy emotionally) you will be in the position to make them want the solution you're offering. Now that puts you in a strong negotiating position doesn't it?

2. What outcomes or transformations do your prospects want to experience by buying your products or services?
I will explain this in more detail in just a moment, but you really have to understand how what you're offering will change your prospects life.

3. How would your prospect finish the following sentence?
'If I could just…?'

What is it that your prospect really wants, what are their

stumbling blocks and how can you remove them? Because when you understand this you will be in a very powerful position to make an irresistible offer that puts you into a great negotiating position.

While Dave Dee explains there is a hierarchy of persuasion in sales there is a similar one in negotiation — it's the same as you put together an irresistible offer to the party you're negotiating with.

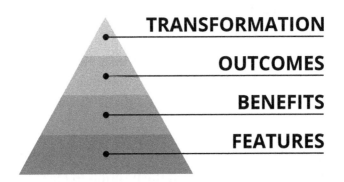

TRANSFORMATION

OUTCOMES

BENEFITS

FEATURES

1. **Features.** At the lowest level are features and when you think about it most salespeople tell you about the features of their product or service. The car salesman will tell you that their car has an eight-cylinder engine, can reach hundred kilometres per hour in 10 seconds and has the latest IT integrated so that you can plug your iPhone, these are the features.

2. **Benefits.** These are what the features mean to you.

Continuing with the car example, while the feature is that the vehicle has an airbag, the benefit is that the airbag will keep you alive if you have an accident.

Of course, features and benefits are well known to all salespeople as basic sales technique, but to be a power salesperson, an influential negotiator you must move up the hierarchy to two even more important levels:

3. **Outcomes.** When you put these benefits together you can reach the next level — the outcome that somebody is going to achieve. Most salespeople never reach this level, however you're going to take your influence to the top level by offering your prospects a transformation.

4. **Transformations.** This is how your prospect's life will change after using your product or service. How they will feel different — that's what you need to tap in to.

Let me explain this in more detail by using an example of one of the services provided by my team at Metropole — amongst other wealth and property services, we provide financial planning advice as some of our team members are licensed financial advisers.

- A **feature** of this particular service would be the adviser could provide his clients with access to a variety of great financial products.
- The **benefit** would be these products would provide a safe haven for our clients to put their money and grow their wealth.
- And **outcome** could be that our client would be able to retire without being dependent upon the government or a pension.
- But the way our financial planners can influence prospects to use their services is to discuss the **transformation** they would achieve which is that our prospects

will be able to live the golden years the way they want to.

But first we need to find out what our prospects actually want to achieve because only then can we tailor our sales presentation towards that.

In other words, we diagnose what our client's needs are before prescribing a solution. That puts us in a much better position of influence because we are giving them what they want because everyone wants something a little different. Some may want to vacation and cruise around the world, others may want to downsize and live near the water, yet others want to leave a legacy for their family.

So ask good questions aimed at uncovering the real need or problem your customer has. Listen attentively to the answers. Never assume that you know already.

Now before you look at this and say, *'this doesn't apply to me, I tend to sell or negotiate business to business and therefore an emotional and personal transformation won't make a difference'*, remember you are never really selling business to business. You're selling to a group, a person, or group of people in the business that not only care about the business but have their own personal agenda which could include impressing their superior at work.

In the next chapter I'll explain another way of 'getting inside the head' of those you wish to persuade, and that's by using hypnotic language.

HOW TO USE LANGUAGE TO HYPNOTISE YOUR PROSPECTS

■ ■ ■

Imagine if you had the power to influence people's subconscious minds.

Imagine if you could do it by using simple trigger words to activate involuntary hypnotic 'reflexes' in their brains.

Now imagine you could use this power to help you become a more persuasive influencer.

You probably don't believe this can actually happen, but it can.

So let's start with a bit of an explainer, just in case you may be thinking that I'm about to teach you a bunch of tricks that will hold other people under your spell in the same way that a hypnotist makes people dance around on stage like chickens.

That is not the case at all, as fun as that sounds. But, and this is a very big but, what I am about to teach you is just as powerful. You won't need to put people to sleep to get them to do what you want because you'll understand language tricks to help you dramatically improve your persuasive power.

Make no mistake about it: the words we use are very, very powerful. In fact, I have already used them in this chapter to keep you reading.

You see…using the right word or phrase at the right time can make the difference between a deal or no deal, a signature on the dotted line or a client who walks away. How would you like to know how to use some special words, a few key phrases or a few strategic sentences that could help you become more persuasive?

This kind of language is what is referred to as hypnotic language and the beauty is that you can use these words in a one on one selling or negotiating situation, you can use it in one on many selling (such as in emails, on stage or on webinars) and you can also use it in your personal life to become more powerfully, personally persuasive.

But let's be clear…this is not about tricking people. I'm not suggesting you use these techniques to manipulate someone into buying products or services that they don't want or need, or if they're not going to get the results they desire. It's about helping people who would benefit from your products or services and doing it in a sophisticated, non salesy way.

What is hypnotic language?

Well, hypnotic language isn't about hypnotising people, but it does rely on the same principle of accessing people's unconscious minds. Essentially this means you use language to appeal to a part of people they're not aware of.

NLP teaches us that particular words, phrases, and patterns of speech shoot past the conscious mind's 'guardians' and dive straight into the subconscious. These words influence people because they allow you to reach the part of the mind that actually controls decision making.

Amazing, huh? This language tells your prospect, in a very subtle way, what they should think and do by the suggestive language you use.

Remember I mentioned Milton Erickson the psychiatrist when I discussed NLP before. He used language in a very deliberate way in his work and was renowned for his gift at using words to conjure certain responses in people. In fact, many people were put in a trance by his expert use of language.

Now I'm going to suggest that the desired goal of all salesmen and women is to put their prospect in a trance. I know this may sound a bit airy fairy, but we all go into trances at times. Think about those moments in the day when a certain memory will provoke you to stare into the middle distance before someone interrupts your dream-like state! Or, think about when someone particularly boring talks to you and you find your eyes glazing over and your mind drifting. This is a gift all on its own.

I then learned that this was also the method used by mentalists who didn't really have mythical powers but were really just magicians. David Dee (www.DaveDee.com), who started as a magician and is now an expert sales trainer, has written a lot about hypnotic language. I'll be using some of his examples, as well as some of my own, to arm you with the hypnotic language you can use in negotiations, at home, and with your kids!

And this works because great negotiators know how to put people in a trance — a positive, enjoyable one — by using language to trigger certain emotions, build trust and rapport and prompt you to act. They use words that bypass the other party's mental gatekeepers.

A lot of what is mistaken for charm is really just someone who knows how to use language, both verbal and non-verbal, to get what they want. Think about some of the great speakers of our time: they all used language to persuade others. Barack Obama is a recent example of the skilled persuader. The former US president knows how to phrase language, pause at the right moments and emphasise certain words to create a positive, even moving, experience for his audience.

The best US preachers are also skilled at getting their congregations to follow in their footsteps. How do they do this? Certainly not by forcing them. It's all down to the power of language, which can put people in a trance.

There are many more modern examples of people who have successfully used language to influence others, but I've found that the best way to describe hypnotic language is by showing you what it sounds like.

Let's get started with a number of power words and phrases.

1. IMAGINE

I find using the word 'imagine' bypasses your prospect's natural reaction not to do what you ask them to do. It's our natural reaction to question a request or instruction. To find a reason to disagree with it. The critical mind throws up objections.

What's interesting, though, is this doesn't happen if you just ask someone to *imagine* something. Especially if you ask them to imagine the *outcome* of the sale, rather than making the purchase itself. There's no resistance to that.

By asking your prospect to imagine something, you bypass that critical part of their brain that throws up objections, and 'sneak in' to their mind through the back door of their imagination.

Psychologists tell us that the brain literally cannot tell the difference between *imagining* reality and actually *experiencing* reality. As strange as it may sound, as far as your brain is concerned there's no difference between visualising a house and seeing a house.

Remember — the fear of loss is far stronger than the desire for gain. This means that if you can get your prospect to feel a sense of ownership for your offering, you invoke a much stronger desire than by merely offering benefits. By getting them to imagine *owning* it, *they become as if they already have it.*

As if they have already bought it. And the natural thing to do then is to *keep it*…which means making the purchase.

An example: 'Can you **imagine** what it would be like living in this house. **Imagine yourself** being able to stroll to the shops, the cafes and the train that takes you directly to town. Picture what it would be like to wake up to these sorts of views each morning.'

Even though on the surface 'imagine' may seem to appeal to visually oriented people more than the auditory and kinaesthetic (feeling) people, this works well across all types. The key is to complement the word 'imagine' with a tailored approach when speaking with the auditory or kinaesthetically oriented people. With auditory folk, you could say to say, 'Can you imagine what it would be like living in this house, hearing the birds chirping early in the morning and the sound of the ocean waves?' With the kinaesthetic people, you want to say, 'Can you imagine what it would be like living in this house, as you can touch and feel the premium finishes throughout the house?'

2. BECAUSE

Did you know that a sentence doesn't have to make sense for you to believe it, because we know that a sentence with a certain word allows us to trick your mind into thinking it's a reasonable sentence?

Just read that sentence again and you'll see it's really two disconnected statements that I've joined together with the word *because*.

A sentence doesn't have to make sense for you to believe it. The word because turns these two unconvincing statements into one convincing one. You probably didn't internally think 'why is that?' when you read that sentence, because I gave you a reason. That reason may not make sense on its own, but when I combine the two thoughts together they can easily bypass your critical mind.

The word because is a very powerful word in the art of persuasion, because it works.

When our mind's gatekeeper hears that word, it treats it as a cue to let the next part of the conversation (or writing or email) through to the unconscious mind.

This is expertly illustrated by Robert Cialdini in his book *Influence: The Psychology of Persuasion*, which I mentioned before.

He cites a study where at a university the experimenter asked to push in line at the library to photocopy some papers:

'Excuse me, I have five pages. May I use the copy machine because I'm in a rush?'
The number of people who agreed: 94%.

'Excuse me, I have five pages. May I use the copy machine?'
The number of people who agreed: 60%.

You'd be inclined to think the difference was because of the reason she gave. But a further experiment indicated otherwise...

'Excuse me, I have five pages. May I use the copy machine because I have to make some copies?'
The number of people who agreed: 93%.

Notice that no real reason was given this time — obviously, *everyone* waiting for the copy machine had to make copies. Yet nearly as many people agreed as when a real reason was given.

How can you start using this hypnotic word to increase your influence?

3. YOU

You is a hypnotic word because it's a placeholder for your name. We all like to hear our name. But it has to be used correctly.

I'm sure you regularly received marketing emails with subject lines like, 'Johnathan, top 10 property hotspots'. And many emails you get will start with your first name; long ones will include it several times.

The problem is, this approach *doesn't work* anymore. You immediately think 'This doesn't feel right' because no one but a marketer would email you like that.

You may have experienced the same thing from telemarketers. You'll find their script always has them saying your name, as if it will build rapport, but it actually just feels creepy since they don't know you.

But the word *you* or *your* is different. It's more natural to use in conversation, so you don't need to worry about being heavy-handed. Yet it has the same basic power as using your own name.

Again, when people talk about us, we tend to be lulled into a sense of security and the words bypass the mind's gatekeeper and stimulate the unconscious mind.

An example: At Metropole we help you build your wealth faster and safer than the average investor allowing you to grow, protect and pass on your wealth to your family without incurring the risks the average investor faces.

4. DID YOU KNOW

Did you know that many people don't realise how easy it is to slip a thought past your critical mind?

Framing a statement as a truth using *did you know* or other suggestive phrasing encourages you to treat it as true. As you may have begun to realise, it's a matter of perspective.

If I tell you 'buying shares is a great investment', you may recoil as your conscious mind judges whether or not my statement is actually true. However, if I tell you that 'most people don't realise how easy it is buy shares that make great long-term investments', you can begin to accept it as true without thinking through the reasons why or why not it is true.

The secret is that when I say 'some people think' or 'most people don't know' or 'experts agree' you subconsciously embrace the truth of the statement before you begin to question it. This guides you toward embracing my ideas, even when you wouldn't naturally accept them.

Other similar phrases you could use include: 'As you know...' 'As you might be aware...' 'As you might have heard...'

'Obviously…'

When you say these words, you instantly make your prospect become aware of that fact, even if they weren't aware of this before you made the statement.

An example using the expression 'as you may already be aware': 'As you may already be aware, this suburb has had significant capital growth in the order of around 10% per annum for the last decade.'

This phrase makes it very likely the other party will accept your statement that buying a property in this location is a good idea considering its strong capital growth potential.

An example using the word 'obviously':
'Obviously we'll need to establish what happens in the event that you don't finish the building works specified in the contract on time…'

Whenever you hear the word *obviously* in a negotiation, know that something that was not obvious is coming your way.

5. YES

I'm sure you've heard that it's good to get your prospect to say *yes* when you're trying to persuade them. And the more often they say yes in a conversation the more you build up a positive expectancy and this helps you get your foot in the door.

The more yeses, the wider the door opens. The more yeses, the higher your chance of persuading your prospect.

Now, a little bit earlier I explained how using the words 'obviously' or 'naturally' before a statement that you want your prospect to agree with makes them say 'yes' — even if it's only in their mind.

Then there's the standard ones from sales books, when you add 'Isn't it?' 'Wasn't she?' 'Shouldn't he?' or 'Don't you agree?' at the end of a statement.

The problem with that is a lot of people know those strategies. Therefore, the key is, when you want your prospect to say yes throughout your discussion to mix it up a bit. You can't use the same strategies over and over to get them to say yes.

Here are some questions you could ask. First make a statement, then ask one of these questions and it will get your prospect to say yes.

- *'Do you agree with me?'* And if you add a slight nod of your head when you ask this question, you're going to get a yes response almost every time.
- *'So would it be fair to say* that having whiter teeth and a brighter smile makes you more attractive?'
- *'Do you sometimes find that…?'* and then whatever it is for your product or service that you want them to agree with. Or *'Let me ask you this. Do you sometimes find that…?'*
- *'Does this sound like something you've heard before?'*

Another really simple strategy to get your prospect to say yes is to simply make a statement and end with, *OK?* 'Just lift up this tennis racquet and see how light it is. OK, Jarrod?'

6. THE FALSE CHOICE

Of course you can choose whether or not you want to use this type of hypnotic language in your daily conversation to become more persuasive. Some people aren't ready to accept that people are easy to manipulate, which is just fine for them.

While the above statement, on its face, is pure choice, it's actually not. I state that you have some options, that you can make a choice, but before you can make a choice you have to accept what I'm saying into your mind. Once the thought is in there, I can guide you toward accepting it by suggesting that the only real reason you wouldn't make the choice I want you to make is because you're just not ready, or you're too stupid, or something else that you don't want to be true. Your mind betrays itself.

That's why using this tactic, the appearance of a choice that isn't really there, is so powerful.

As children we were all exposed to 'all the cool kids are doing *xyz*' or 'only losers do *xyz*'. While a choice is technically there, you only really want to choose the course of action that makes you cool, and you don't want to do something that makes you a loser. It's a false choice, because your desires override your critical thinking.

The subconscious *always* beats the conscious mind. Always.

7. LINKING TWO UNRELATED STATEMENTS

Basically, the premise behind this technique is that you make two unrelated statements, but then you tie those two unrelated statements together forming what sounds like a logical conclusion and that is the conclusion that you want your prospect to reach.

Imagine your prospect doesn't believe your product or service will deliver the results that you know it will, you could drop a seemingly innocuous statement such as:

'Despite all the proof that our product does delivers xyz, there are still some people who don't believe it. Well, of course, John there are still some people that don't believe we landed on the moon either.'

Now, this will get your prospect to chuckle, but in reality it causes them to automatically believe what you just said because, if they don't believe what you just said, you're comparing them to someone who believes something ridiculous.

This is a great technique when your competition makes outrageous and possibly false claims. I would never name them, but I'd say something like...

'As you might be aware, there are some people claiming that you can lose 7kg in two weeks without doing any exercise and without changing your diet at all. Well, of course, John there are still some people that don't believe we landed on the moon either.'

'Amazingly, some people claim you can buy an investment property with no money down. Of course, some people believe in the Easter Bunny, as well.'

So, what you're doing there is comparing someone who believes outrageous claims your competition is suggesting, or maybe even your industry in general is saying, such as that they can lose 7kg in two weeks without have to change their diet at all or without having to do any exercise, to someone who believes in the Easter Bunny. Of course, that's ridiculous.

8. WORDS THAT WILL GET THEM TO TALK

By now you know great persuaders are great listeners. They're good at asking questions to elicit the outcome and the desires their prospect wants and then really, really listening to the answers.

In order to do that though, your prospect must participate. If they won't volunteer information, it's going to be difficult for you to negotiate with them.

However, when you're dealing with someone who understands a little about negotiation they may not be forth-coming. They know that if they tell you what they really want, what they really desire, the outcome that they want to achieve that once you know that you're probably going to try to sell them something. And although they want the result, they're afraid to tell you because they're hesitant about making a commitment.

The 'We can make you talk' script is the solution to this. And you want to use this solution, this script, at the very, very beginning of your presentation before you start asking the diagnostic questions, the questions that dig deep into what your prospect really desires.

Here's a little script that should help open up the conversation. Of course you'll change the words to suit your situation, but try and keep the same structure.

'I've been in this business for over 10 years so *naturally* I know a lot about financial planning.'

'*Obviously* as a personal trainer, I know a lot about how to make you fitter and slimmer.'

Using the key word 'naturally' or 'obviously' gets your prospect to give instant agreement.

Then you continue with, 'So perhaps you could talk a little bit more about where you are right now, about what you want to achieve, then we can talk about some options we could put together for you. Sound good?'

Notice how many times I use the word 'you'. Again, this seems like it's nothing, but this wording is immensely powerful.

Rather than being a salesperson you're becoming an advisor using 'you, you, you' and focussing on them. You're sounding friendly and this should open up your prospect to share their thoughts with you.

Then, slowly you transition to, 'we' which a powerful form of persuasion and influence...

'We will develop a plan for helping you achieve your financial goals.'

'Together we will get you fitter.'

'We can do this together.'

Isn't that different to 'I'll give you a plan so you can achieve your financial goals'?

Then I follow with a phrase along these lines: 'So, let me ask you. If you could wave a magic wand and it's three months from now (or three years from now), what would have to happen for you to be happy...?' or some similar phrase to elicit the outcome is that they're looking for.

When you use a statement like this and they answer your question, the other party has to look into the future, and when they look into the future, they're painting a picture in their mind of their ideal scenario and they're linking that to you. In NLP that is called 'future pacing'.

So, they experience the result in advance, on some level, because in order to answer that question they've got to picture how perfect it would be, and when they picture it in their mind, they experience an emotion inside their body. When they experience the emotion inside their body, that is linked to you and what a great position to be in.

A clever use of words

The *Feel, Felt, Found* technique is a proven, simple framework of using clever words to handle objections. It's something I use all the time and goes like this:

1. I tell the other party that 'I understand how you feel'. This is intended to tell them that you have heard them and can empathise.
2. I tell them about someone else who felt the same way initially. Here I'm telling the other party that they are not alone, and that things can change.
3. Then I tell them how that person found that when they did what you wanted/bought the product they got what they wanted.

Finally, I ask permission to push back. 'Would it be helpful to explore some of the things I've learned working with other people in similar situations?'

The principle behind this is that you should never argue whenever you receive an objection. If you do the other negotiator feels honour bound to defend their point of view. So rather than arguing, calmly use this technique.

In order to craft 'Feel, Felt, Found' word patterns effectively, you have to accurately identify what it is that the person is feeling or believing and identify something else they want or believe that is more empowering or useful for what was 'found'.

Effectively you are building a bridge from the objection to a more useful expectation. The belief or desire in the 'found' section has to be important to your prospect for this pattern to work. If they don't value it, if it doesn't close the gap you've created, your word patterns will have no power.

Sometimes it is worth personalising the 'found' example with real life statistics and figures relevant to your prospect, so that they can form a clearer, sharper picture of exactly what they could gain if they go with your product or service.

Here's how you could use this:

Objection: Your prices are too high.

Feel: 'I get where you're coming from. If I were in your shoes, I would want to make sure I got the most value for every dollar spent. It makes sense to me that you want to use your money in the best way possible.'

Felt: 'We've had clients who were initially concerned about our prices as well. Clearly, we're not the cheapest option out there.'

Found: 'What our clients have found is that after using our services/product etc. for six months their return on investment was far greater than they expected and the solutions were nowhere near as difficult to implement as they expected, so they discovered that the price point is actually a great value because their ROI is so excellent.

Permission: 'Would you mind if I take a few minutes to explain how this worked for them and see if that might be something that could work for you?'

Objection: Your competition seems to have a better solution.

Feel: 'Thanks for sharing that concern with me, I understand how you feel. It makes total sense to me that you are evaluating all the other options out there.'

Felt: 'I am the same way: when I buy a product, I always want to try to make the best decision given all of the different options. In fact, I know many of our existing long-term clients felt the same way when they were initially evaluating their options before working with us.'

Felt: 'What I've found is that the best decision isn't just about the quality or features, but it involves all aspects including price, post purchase service, and even some intangibles, like user experience.'

Permission: 'Would you mind if we spent a few minutes going back over the different aspects of what you need to see if we can come up with a combined package that would work for you?'

Objection: I like the idea of an electric car, but the technology is new and I'm not sure where I can charge it.

Feel: 'You know, I understand exactly how you feel.'

Felt: 'You might be surprised to learn that a lot of other clients I talk to felt exactly the same way — people who are now driving our cars.'

Found: 'I say that because after they started looking into the reasons for their feelings, the same ones you expressed, they found that this technology is now tried and proven with over half a million electric cars on the road and even though you can charge your car at home overnight, there are now over 150,000 charging stations throughout the state. This is probably all just a rumour started by petrol companies isn't it?'

Think about it, your potential purchaser would be much more inclined to consider your electric car now wouldn't they?

The principle of Feel, Felt, Found is to agree with the other party until they agree with you.

Another clever use of words

A powerful turn of phrase I learned in the book *The Ultimate Book of Influence* by Chris Helder, an outstanding speaker on the topic of communication and influence, is what Chris calls — positive, *positive, positive, negative.*

Since I've learned this, I've taught it to my team and we use it regularly in verbal as well as written communication with clients and prospects.

The way it works is that first we reinforce three positive messages (in areas that are important to the other party) and then deliver a 'whammy' by creating a negative that would occur if they didn't take advantage of the opportunity you are offering them.

I often use this method when encouraging clients to come to our high-end five-day $10,000 Wealth Retreat that we hold annually on the Gold Coast. I genuinely believe that many of our clients should attend because I have seen the outcomes and transformations this five-day intensive event has had on delegates who end up making massive changes to their personal, business and financial lives. Yet when I recommend joining us prospects are often reluctant to give up five days of work and $10,000. (Maybe I haven't created a big enough gap!)

I say something along the lines of:

Congratulations, you've spent years building a substantial property portfolio (**positive**), you've got great cash flow from your business (**positive**), and you clearly have the desire to take your investments to the next level — that's why you consulted me (**positive**). Wouldn't it be a shame if you didn't take advantage of the opportunity to network with a great group of attendees at Wealth Retreat and spend time with our faculty who will be able to show you how to take your investments to the next level and help you build the financial independence you desire (**negative**)?

As you can see, I have built the prospects up with three positive messages and then I've delivered a negative message outlining the gap (causing pain.) This is a great way to convince people to take action.

Clearly you bought this book because you want to become a better negotiator, you've taken the time and trouble to learn some new ideas on how to become more influential, you are being introduced to some new principles of persuasion. Wouldn't it be a shame if you didn't put these into practice and become the power negotiator you want to be?

See what I did? This principle works just as well in the written word or in emails as you have just seen.

So now you understand how hypnotists do it

Of course, none of this is 'magic' if you know the secret. Sure, it will take a bit of practice but soon you'll be able to close more deals or influence more people by having them under your spell.

And since you're now aware of some of these hypnotic words and phrases, you will probably start to see them used everywhere. That gives you a slight edge over everyone else, because being aware of hypnotic language allows you to build up defences against the subconscious power of those words and patterns.

You can either choose to use these techniques and become more persuasive, or not. It's entirely your choice. Just remember, use your new power wisely!

In the next chapter we'll look at a few things you should NOT say in a negotiating setting.

9 THINGS YOU SHOULD NEVER SAY IN A NEGOTIATION

■ ■ ■

There are some phrases so powerful that they can turn a negotiation around. One that wasn't going well can be put on track with the careful insertion of a word or phrase as I've just explained.

Then there are those that have the opposite effect. Like a metaphorical bomb being thrown, they blow up all the hard work you did during the negotiation phase and put you, the negotiator, in a losing position.

People accidentally say these phrases all the time when negotiating but they rarely realise the full extent of what it is they're communicating to the other person.

When training my team at Metropole, I make sure they're aware of the power of certain phrases and that they make sure they avoid them during negotiations.

So what are these phrases? Here are some of the most common ones to avoid.

1. YOU'RE NOT MAKING SENSE

Ah, what a great one this is! Nothing will alienate the other person faster than an insult. You may be frustrated, and the other person may genuinely not make any sense, but never bring attention to the other negotiator's shortfalls, otherwise you can kiss that deal goodbye.

It's also up to you to understand what another person is saying. After all, your job as a negotiator is to get a clear idea of what it is they're trying to communicate, both verbally and non-verbally.

You need to ask the right questions to gain that understanding, so if you don't understand what someone is saying, well, part of that is on you.

2. I DON'T AGREE

Saying you don't agree with what the other party is saying or thinking will get you nowhere. If you argue with their logic you are more likely than not to end up in deadlock. You have to recognise that both of you have your own positions and you're seeing things from different perspectives.

Instead use the FEEL, FELT, FOUND strategy I mentioned in the last chapter — it's a great way to handle objections.

3. YOU'LL REGRET THIS

While this phrase may not be as openly insulting as the ones above, it's still going to put the other party off-side. Once again: the other person may live to regret the decision they make, but that is not up to you to point out.

Very few people would react well to a statement like this and all they will end up regretting is having started negotiations with you in the first place!

4. SHOULD WE MEET IN THE MIDDLE?

You'll hear this said a lot during your time as a negotiator, but never, ever use the words yourself. The concept of meeting in the middle or splitting the difference usually does not serve you well. All it represents is halfway between what you think is reasonable and what the other party wants.

You need to anchor the price from the get-go — high, but not insultingly high — and then negotiate to what you're comfortable with from there.

5. I MAKE THE FINAL CALL

At the beginning of many negotiations, someone will typically ask, 'Who makes the decisions?'

Now that may very well be you, but it's a bad idea to own up to it. Sounds odd right? Well, remember how we spoke before of the need to reference another power — a higher power — who you need to check everything with? It could be an investor, a partner, or your business partner.

The idea behind this move is that it enables you to buy some time. Time is everything in high-stakes negotiations and often deals that are presented a certain way look better than they actually are upon reflection.

If you can buy yourself time to consult with a mystery decision-maker then you will reduce the risk of signing up to something that on first blush seemed like a good deal, but in fact isn't.

6. GET STUFFED

Negotiations can be extremely frustrating at times and it makes sense that there will be moments that you really want to let off some steam and let someone know where they can stick it.

Don't. Nothing is more undermining of your personal authority quite like resorting to abuse. If you tell someone where to go, you can rest assured that the story won't just stay with them, but will spread like wildfire through your professional networks. This could be very damaging to your career.

You may find yourself negotiating with someone who has a short fuse and tells YOU where to go. This does not give you a free pass to fire back at them.

Always respond to attack with respect and courtesy. At the very least, it will annoy the other person that they were not able to get a rise out of you.

7. THIS IS MY FINAL OFFER

Whatever you do, try not to back yourself or others into a corner. Only use this phrase if you truly mean it and are prepared to follow through. Although it's often very tempting to respond with this remark, if either party has their back against the wall, it's unlikely you'll arrive at a mutually satisfying conclusion.

8. LET'S WORK OUT THE DETAILS LATER

There's a reason they say the devil's in the details. You wouldn't hire a builder to build your new home without knowing the specifications, the finishes and the fittings. Similarly, you shouldn't agree to a price without under- standing exactly what your prospect expects you to provide.

In an extensive negotiation it's wise to write down the details as the negotiation unfolds and get the other party to confirm these at the end of the negotiation.

Amateur negotiators often make the mistake of getting too excited at the fleeting appearance of agreement at the end of the negotiation and blurt out 'Let's work out the details later', only to find out to their horror that things fall apart afterwards. Remember the first historic meeting between Donald Trump and Kim Jong Un? You don't want to be the guy who publicly broadcast a victory on Twitter, only to find out afterwards that it was all shambles.

Consequently, you need to be wary of the other party who appears hasty in wrapping up a negotiation and dismissively saying 'Don't worry, we'll take care of the details later'. Agreeing to this prematurely will open up a can of worms down the track.

9. DON'T USE AGGRESSIVE, ACCUSATORY LANGUAGE

Don't let the tension or stress of a negotiation show. How you communicate during a negotiation can divulge a lot about your willingness to cooperate.

Instead of saying 'I', emphasise your willingness to work together by using 'we' statements and empathetic phrasing that acknowledges how the other side feels.

Be diplomatic when asking questions. Rather than saying 'Why did you make that choice?' or 'How did you come to that conclusion?', which could make the other person guarded and escalate tensions during a negotiation, opt for more open-ended questions.

Asking 'What led you to make that choice?' invites the other side to explain their reasoning, rather than defending their actions.

As you can see, in negotiations, what you don't say can be as important as what you do say.

I hope you can see a common thread evolving as we discuss how to become an influential negotiator and persuader. You have to understand how the other party thinks and how they communicate. But there's more. You need to understand how you're hard wired, which is what I discuss in the next chapter.

UNDERSTANDING WHY YOU BEHAVE IRRATIONALLY WHEN NEGOTIATING

■ ■ ■

Now that you understand the importance of using the right words and phrases when communicating with others I'm going to take it up a level by teaching you about psychological tendencies that cause the brain to draw incorrect conclusions.

This persuasion stuff is getting a little bit complicated isn't it? But if you want to become an influencer or a power negotiator you are going to have to stop you holding yourself back.

What do I mean by that?

Well…when it comes to negotiating we can sometimes be our own worst enemy. It's not because of the decisions we make, the opportunities we consider or the sales or purchases we miss out on, but rather, it's due to the way we think.

That's because we're subject to cognitive biases — the way our brains sneakily convince us to make decisions that aren't always in our best interests. Cognitive biases may convince us to spend more, save less, and feel more confident in our decisions than perhaps we should.

And the scary thing is, for the most part, we're powerless against them because we never question them. We're not even aware of them most of the time.

Basically a cognitive bias is a shortcut our brain has learned to take because we make thousands of decisions every day and we usually make these decisions with almost no thought, using heuristics, which is a fancy way of describing those shortcut techniques to make snap decisions, such as rules of thumb, educated guesses, profiling, etc.

The world is complicated and if we had to make a perfect decision every time, we'd be so bogged down that we'd never do anything.

We've evolved to use cognitive biases that function as kind of a shortcut to help us make decisions that suit us in the short-term. However, as a negotiator you need to think beyond the short-term and that means tactically using your awareness of cognitive bias to make you a much better negotiator.

In short, if you want to become a better negotiator you'll have to understand how our minds work. So let's look at 10 of these biases so you can understand what I'm getting at.

1. CONFIRMATION BIAS

The best way to sum up confirmation bias is like this: We only see the world we look for. I guess we don't see the world as it is, we see the world as we are.

Interesting thought, isn't it? In other words, we tend to search for information that confirms our view of the world and we ignore what doesn't fit. Think about the news you consume or watch. Most people listen to outlets that reflect their view or politics and the world, and don't tend to venture beyond that comfort zone.

In an uncertain world, we love to be right and we love to be unchallenged because it helps us make sense of things.

We do this automatically, without realising it. Partly because it's easier to see where new pieces fit into the picture puzzle we are working on, rather than imagining a new picture.

The effect of confirmation bias was clearly illustrated in a study with Harvard Business School students.

The students were divided into two groups that were negotiating over a dispute for the claimant's and the defendant's side. Both groups were given common information and confidential instructions. However, the two groups did not know that their confidential instructions were the same. When they were asked to give their assessments of the amounts they could claim on behalf of their party, both groups came up with very different assessments.

This was because, the students were interpreting the information in a way that supported their perspectives, while ignoring information relevant to the other side's claims.

I see this all the time in property investors who believe that a particular type of property or a specific region will make for good investing, then they tend to only seek out news and information that supports that position. Confirmation bias also prevents them from looking objectively at an investment they have already made.

Once we've bought a property we look for information to confirm that we've made a good investment while as the same time ignoring information that may indicate the investment may be a questionable one.

Negotiating takeaway:
Expert negotiators are aware of this fundamental bias and set in place checks and balances to counter it. They recognise that it's easy to analyse the negotiation purely from their own perspective, so they try and walk in the shoes of their counterpart and see things from their perspective.

I read that at an annual general meeting of Berkshire Hathaway held in 2013, the world's most successful investor, Warren Buffet, famously invited David Kass, an ardent critic of Buffett investment philosophy, to present his views on the way Berkshire Hathaway was being run. This was to counter any confirmation bias that might have been influencing Buffet's decisions. If Warren Buffett is big-hearted enough to be open to have his assumptions challenged, perhaps you should too.

As an investor, one way to counter confirmation bias is to read things you're going to disagree with. In other words, read all you can from reputable sources, whether it's confirming your original view or not. Another is to look for reasons your strategies could be wrong, rather than right. In other words, interrogate your assumptions.

In his book *Principles*, Ray Dalio taught that the single most important quality that successful people possess is open-mindedness. They are almost fanatical in their open-mindedness that they actively seek another person's view that may challenge or contradict their own assumptions in the hope of learning something new. In other words, they are totally aware of the presence of confirmation bias and open to being challenged and questioned.

2. ANCHORING BIAS

We have a tendency to use mental 'anchors' or reference points to make decisions and evaluations, and sometimes these lead us astray. Anchoring is the tendency to give too much weight to the first number put on the table in any given deal, and then fail to adjust from that starting point.

It explains why you'll pay $6 for parking after seeing $10 at a car park down the street. The first number you see acts as an anchor and it impacts how you see the figures that follow it.

You can then see how a high anchor influences you to spend more than you normally would.

Property marketers, estate agents and car salespeople use this principle all the time. They start with a high asking price and then you feel good when you extract a discount from them.

This is because the initial price you set for a house, car or for a deal of any kind, exerts a huge influence over negotiations. Whether we like it or not, our minds keep referring back to that initial number.

And this principle is not restricted to numbers or money, it can be about quality too. The best real estate agents know to save the best property they'll show you until last. That is, they show inferior properties first and only show the best one last. That way, potential buyers will appreciate that property much more. By the way, the same thing applies to the Oscars awards ceremony too. Why do you think they keep the pre- sentation of the Best Actor and Best Actress awards to the very last moment?

An example of anchoring

You know how in many restaurants there is a line on the glass so the waiter knows how much wine to pour into your glass and not give you more than you pay for? Well the other day we went to an expensive restaurant and ordered drinks with our meals and the waiter poured our wine — a glass of red for Pam and some white Moscato for me (I prefer sweets wines). The wine glasses were on the large side and there was no pouring line on them. I said to Pam, *'I think he's short changed me — it doesn't look like he's given me my fair share.'* Remember I had a different shape glass to Pam. No, the waiter probably didn't but I had nothing concrete to 'anchor' my expectations to. In fact, I probably received a fair share of wine.

Imagine if this restaurant did etch little lines on their glasses and the waiter poured a bit more into the glass so I felt I'd 'won', that I got a bit more than my fare share because I'd anchored my expectation to what the measure on the glass said. I would have been a much happier customer and more likely to give him a tip because he'd pre anchored my expectations.

Another example of anchoring

This technique is called 'asking for more'. Here's how it works…

Let's say you want a friend to donate $100 to your favourite charity, but for them $100 is a significant sum of money. Instead of asking for less, I suggest you ask them for $250, saying that that's what most people are giving to this charity. If they don't want to donate $250, make it easier for them and say 'That's okay, let's just be content with a $100 donation, that'll still do a lot of good.' Your friend will be relieved to save $150 and give you 'only' $100, considering you anchored the figure of $250 in their mind.

Children are very good at using this technique, aren't they? They always ask for a lot up front and are then happy to accept a compromise. They ask to go to expensive holiday destinations and when their parents say they can't afford it the children ask, 'OK can we go to the movies?' The kids get what they want, and the parents feel the pressure has been taken off them.

This also calls in one of Dr Cialdini's principles — the feeling of obligation to reciprocate the concession you initially gave. People will be more receptive to grant you your true and smaller request after they have declined your first and bigger one. They will feel embarrassed to turn down a second favour, especially if it's much easier to comply with than your first request. Often they feel a sense of guilt for refusing your first request and if your second request is something they can do or afford they grab the opportunity to make it up to you.

Negotiating takeaway

How can you use the concept I just mentioned in your business? It's just another of way of under promising and over delivering.

It's natural for our brain to rely on an anchor as a shortcut when making decisions.

When your counterpart has dropped an anchor, the first step is to recognise the move, since you can't defend against something that you don't see occurring.

Next, you need to defuse the anchor by saying something like: 'I'm not trying to play games with you, but we are miles apart on price.' That puts you in charge of the ballpark figure, and not the other way around.

A common mistake is to respond with a counteroffer before defusing the other side's anchor. If the other party opens with $100, and you want to counter with $50 before presenting your offer, you need to make clear that $100 is unacceptable. If you don't first defuse the anchor, you are implying that $100 is a reasonable starting price.

3. LOSS AVERSION

Loss Aversion refers to our tendency to prefer avoiding losses over making equivalent gains.

This means that most people would rather not lose $100 than gain $100. Why is this so?

Psychologists tell us that the pain of losing is psychologically about twice as powerful as the pleasure of gaining. People are more willing to take risks (or even behave dishonestly) to avoid a loss than to make a gain.

Let's look at two examples so you can understand the importance of this principle and then use it to your full advantage.

Firstly, let's analyse a study that was conducted on two groups of participants waiting in line outside a theatre. One group had been waiting for 45 minutes and the other for around 15 minutes, when they were both informed that they would have to wait for an additional 30 minutes before being let into the theatre. The group that had waited for 45 minutes continued to wait for the additional half an hour while many of those from the 15-minute group chose to leave rather than waiting longer.

The second oft-quoted example comes from the Harvard Business School. Apparently, every year in his negotiation classes, Professor Max Bazerman auctions off a $20 note to his students.

The auction's rules are simple: The winner pays the amount of the bid and 'wins' the $20. The loser pays the amount of the losing bid.

In his auction, generally, most students drop out at about $16 or $17. They see a bargain if they win, but if they come in second, they're willing to pay a nominal amount.

Every year there are always a couple of students who continue on the path they started, they become loss averse because to drop out would mean that they have to pay their last bid. This means the bidding always continues way above $20, meaning the winner will pay more to win the auction than the prize is worth. The leading bidder keeps bidding while the underbidder continues to raise their bid because losing is a 'deeply unattractive option'. Therefore the option of continuing to bid is relatively attractive.

Apparently the final bid often gets quite high.

What both of these examples highlight is that, once invested, we do not want to walk away empty-handed. If something is in our sights, and it slips away from us, our aversion to loss will kick in and we will often go to extraordinary lengths to 'win' whatever is under threat.

Negotiating takeaway

When we have spent resources on something — whether it is as small as waiting in line for a movie, or as significant as a property investment that is underperforming — we're inclined to stay the course so as not to waste what we've already spent. In other words, we want to avoid feeling the loss of what's been spent (time, money, emotion) so we hang in there hoping for a gain, even when sometimes that just leads to a bigger loss in the long run. When negotiating, many of us can be negatively affected by this loss aversion bias and make irrational decisions or take illogical risks to 'protect' an investment which might have better been foregone.

I've seen what many would consider smart businesspeople continue negotiating and reach a less than satisfactory result because they've invested so much time, effort and emotion into the negotiation, rather than starting a new negotiation with a different party.

Similarly, I've seen smart negotiators ensure that the other person invests a lot of time, energy and emotion, knowing they're less likely to drop out of the negotiations and will settle on a deal even if it's not the deal they were hoping for. See how you can use this principle in negotiations?

On a very similar note you should be aware of...

4. SUNK COST FALLACY

Have you ever ordered a meal at a restaurant only to realise halfway through the meal that you aren't that hungry anymore? Yet you want to get your money's worth since you have to pay for the full meal, so you continue to eat even though you're full.

Congratulations! You've just fallen victim to the sunk cost fallacy which occurs when we place value on something because we've already invested time or money in it.

A 'sunk cost' is a cost that has already been incurred and can't be recovered. Of course these costs shouldn't be considered when making financial decisions because they've already been paid, but when they're considered, the decision-maker falls victim to the sunk cost fallacy.

The problem is, once we've invested time and money in an idea, future decisions are more influenced by what we've already done than by what is in front of us.

A great example of this is Nokia, which was the leading mobile phone company of the early 2000s — almost everyone had a Nokia phone. But they fell into the sunk cost trap when new competitors began revolutionising the market. Executive leadership continued to pursue funding Nokia's proprietary (and outdated) operating system, while Apple and Google took over the phone market with new smartphone technology. Nokia couldn't catch up to its new competitors and lost its place as the top brand in the industry.

The sunk cost fallacy can get in the way of your investment success. When it comes to investing, it can be hard to admit you made a bad decision. When a property investment turns out to be a dud, or a share investment loses value, many investors hold on to worthless shares or an underperforming property much longer than they should, losing money and time in the process, rather than changing strategies which may make them feel as though they failed as an investor.

5. STATUS QUO BIAS

This is very similar to the principle of 'Loss Aversion' and describes our tendency to stick with what we know whether or not it's the best course of action. It could be as simple as buying the same name-brand groceries that you always have or as complex as holding on to that underperforming property.

People do this partly because they want to avoid costs, even when it's apparent that those costs will be offset by a larger gain, being the long-term growth of a better performing property.

Many banks, utilities and insurance companies rely on this status quo bias to retain customers. Premiums and costs may go up, and there may be better deals elsewhere, but people often stick with what they know.

Negotiating takeaway

Psychologists have shown that most of us disproportionately stick with the status quo because we often weigh the potential losses from switching from the status quo more heavily than the potential gains.

That's why all the successful investors, businesspeople and entrepreneurs I know have mentors, coaches and mastermind groups to help them see their blind spots and to encourage them to keep moving forward. It is all about accountability.

That's one of the benefits attendees get by joining me and my inner circle at Wealth Retreat each year www.WealthRetreat. com.au They get pushed out of their comfort zone and by gaining a new peer group and a set of unreasonable friends who will be their accountability partners they lose their status quo bias.

Like I write in many of my psychology of success blogs, change and disruption often leads to success, in the long-term, while staying the same will lead to stagnation.

6. INATTENTIONAL BLINDNESS

You're likely to be able to relate to this one. Inattentional blindness is a common cognitive bias and relates to our tendency to see, hear or experience only that which we are focussed on, and to be blind to other obvious factors that is not our focus.

I guess it's the reason why we fail to notice bloopers in movies — we are focusing so hard on the main character and the action, that you might not notice the unexpected, such as the famous Starbucks cup displayed by mistake in the TV series, *Game Of Thrones*.

Similarly, when you are focused on a specific issue in the middle of an intense negotiation, it is likely that you will filter out much of the world around you, especially when you're processing complex issues.

7. BANDWAGON BIAS

This is the psychological phenomenon whereby people do something primarily because other people are doing it and it follows on from Dr. Cialdini's principle of social proof that I've already explained to you.

This tendency of people to align their beliefs and behaviours with those of a group is also called 'herd mentality'. Herding is the phenomenon by which animals and humans herd or stick together as a mechanism to enhance our safety.

This made sense when we were cavemen roaming the plains — staying in the herd with others protected you from being eaten by a sabre-toothed tiger, but it doesn't necessarily make sense today.

The bandwagon effect has wide implications and is commonly seen during strong property markets when the media stirs up a frenzy and hence a property boom is created. That is why it's important to remember that when it comes to financial matters 'the herd' is usually wrong as most property investors or never build a substantial portfolio.

I've seen numerous investment fads and fashions come and go — USA property investing; New Zealand property; time share; mining towns; vendor finance; hot spots etc. — and I've seen many investors caught up in the hype with the mistaken belief that if others are doing it, it must be a good investment.

But as it (always) turns out, the herd in each of these instances was wrong.

And it's much the same with share market booms like the tech boom, or the recent bit coin bubble.

To help avoid the pitfalls of the bandwagon effect, I am reminded of the Robert Frost poem *The Road Not Taken*, where he writes: 'Two roads diverged in a wood and I, I took the one less travelled by, and that has made all the difference.'

Negotiation takeaway

It pays to remember that just because everyone else is doing it, doesn't mean you should follow the crowds. Unfortunately, excellence is the exception rather than the rule and that's why I believe you should aspire to be unique and not part of the herd.

As Warren Buffet said, 'Be fearful when others are greedy and be greedy when others are fearful.'

8. OVERCONFIDENCE

Successful salespeople and businesspeople need to possess a high level of confidence to succeed and meet the many challenges they face, but there is a hazy line that separates being confident in what you do and becoming overconfident.

Overconfidence is one of the worst things that can happen to a negotiator, as you tend to think you're smarter than you are and forget to implement the lessons you're learning in this book. You may have had a few successes, but that should not lead you to discount the worth or the validity of other people's judgment. Once you discount other people, and solely rely on your own intelligence, you're cutting yourself off from a rich pool of information and options necessary for a successful negotiation.

Negotiation takeaway

The best defence against the sort of blindness that comes from overconfidence is to ask questions and be sceptical of your preconceptions, so you can be in the best position to negotiate from a position of objectivity and understanding. Draw on the resources of people around you and be honest about your strengths and weaknesses. Don't take success as a sign that you have nothing left to learn — the opposite is true.

9. PERSONAL HISTORY BIAS

Depending on your experience in life, your viewpoint will influence your attitude towards investing. Research shows that the way you feel about a topic is hard to alter and was most likely shaped by events experienced in your youth.

Someone who grew up in the Great Depression, for instance, would have a much different attitude towards money and investing than someone who grew up in a family that experienced financial prosperity during the 1980s.

These early influences will show up in the risks you're willing to take and the investments that appeal to you.

Negotiation takeaway

A power negotiator will learn as much as they can about the other party to help understand what motivates them and what preconceptions they bring to the table. They'll also be aware of what shaped their own attitudes towards investing.

10. BIAS BIAS

Failing to recognise your many cognitive biases is a bias in itself. Arguably this is the most damaging bias of all, because having blind spots means you're less likely to recognise any of these psychological influences.

When you think you're more objective than you really are, you may be at risk of 'bias bias'.

Negotiation takeaway

The reality is that everyone comes to the negotiating table with their own predispositions and we are all prone to errors in judgment.

The sooner you realise and acknowledge these tendencies in yourself, the more open you will be to improving and making better investment decisions. Simply becoming aware of these biases means half your battle against your own worst enemy — yourself — is won.

The bottom line

We all want to think we're rational and biases are problems for other people.

However, our brains are designed with blind spots and one of their sneaky tricks is to confer on us the comforting delusion that we, personally, do not have any biases.

This is why so many of us are able to be easily persuaded by others who understand how our minds work knowing we're blind to our blindness.

This, of course, if powerful information for you, the negotiator.

By the way…Don't forget to register your copy of this book at www.negotiateinfluencepersuade.com and access all the bonuses waiting for you.

SECTION TWO:

THE RULES OF NEGOTIATION

Now that you understand some of the psychology behind the art of persuasion, in this section I'm going to get into more of the nitty gritty.

I'm going to explain nine sources of power in a negotiation. But first I'll share 27 Rules of Negotiation.

Many years ago I learned from Herb Cohen that when it comes to negotiations, you need to be involved but not too much. And that took a lot of pressure off me because if you are too emotionally involved, you will lose your perspective and make emotional rather than subjective decisions.

Like all games, you must understand the rules. A skilled negotiator understands the structure and stages of negotiation. If you play a game and don't know the rules, how do you know when the game has begun, reached its mid-point, or neared its conclusion? Let's now look at the rules.

But to make things clear, over the years I've learned that to be a power negotiator you need a degree of flexibility rather than trying to follow hard and fast 'rules'. So let's call the concepts I discuss in this section principles, rather than rules or laws.

In many respects, this is the fun part of my book because once you're aware of them, you can use these principles in your own life to get more of what you want. But like I've already explained: I would prefer that you use these concepts for good, rather than aiming for world domination!

I like to think of what you'll learn in these chapters as a cheat sheet to negotiation success. But there is a reason I waited until now to introduce you to them…

If you tried to apply this information without a keen understanding of the different personality types, the power of invisible influence, and the stages of negotiation, they wouldn't be anywhere near as effective.

The Principles
of Negotiation

■ ■ ■

Principle #1
Everything is negotiable

I've come to realise that everything (well...almost everything) in life is negotiable. This does not mean you are always
going to get what you want or win every negotiation, but
you must remember that everything is potentially up for
negotiation.

And this therefore means there's really no such things as
a 'fair price'. Since every price was set by someone, this
means it could be changed by someone else.

The corollary of this is that a 'fair price' is simply what one
person is willing to pay for a service or a product, and this
will differ wildly between different people and their level of
interest in what's on the table.

This means that there is no bottom or ceiling to what
someone will or will not pay. Think about that for a moment.
Now think about all of the times that you have negotiated
based on your pre-conceived notion of what is and isn't fair.

In other words, nothing is 'non-negotiable', so when the other party tells you this, nod politely but don't take them too seriously. All they are telling you is what is important to them, and that's good to know. But I've found non-negotiable items have a habit of becoming negotiable at the end once you've exerted your persuasive influence.

Think about it…what did you ask for your product, service, or fee when you could have asked for more by creating a bigger desire in your customer by showing them how you can fill a gap or need they have and how valuable that would be for them as I discussed in a previous chapter.

As a consumer think about the times you paid the 'sticker price'. Never be intimidated by asking prices even if they are in writing — and never be afraid to ask for a better or more favourable terms. You'll be surprised how quickly people will change the price or terms if you only just ask.

Remember while you may not be able to change the price during a negotiation there are many other factors that could be open to negotiation. If the price is fixed maybe the other party will be flexible with timeframes to completion, finance terms, add ons etc.

Or when negotiating for a pay rise, if your boss won't give you more dollars why not negotiate on other items such as working from home days, flexi time, length of leave or other benefits such as free parking or gym membership.

Principle #2
Be clear on your negotiating goals

Always go into a negotiation with a plan, but don't have a fixed plan — be prepared to be flexible in how you attain it.

Now, you might think this is obvious, but I've found that that most people go into a negotiation without a clear picture of the various options available to them.

Whether I'm a buyer or seller I always ask myself three key questions:

1. What's the best possible outcome?

Let's say I'm looking to purchase an investment property and my research shows the property is worth $900,000 +/- 5% (that's about as accurate as I can get it). The best scenario is a motivated vendor and no other interested buyers, and I could snare if for $850,000.

2. What's my bottom line?

If it's a unique property with something special about it, I'd be prepared to pay full price for this under the competitive conditions of an auction. So my bottom line is I'd pay up to $950,000 to secure something special.

3. What's my plan B?

What am I going to do if I don't reach an agreeable result? It's important to have a fallback position — this gives me power in the negotiation. I'll just find another property.

Of course, I wouldn't broadcast my answers to the first two questions, but I'd definitely tell the selling agent that I have other options available to me — because this puts me in a position of power.

Principle #3
Always have a plan to leave the negotiation

This follows on from my last point. People can smell desperation a mile off. No matter how keen you are to close a particular deal, even if it seems like the deal of a lifetime to you, always, always have a plan to walk away. Have another option available to you.

Think about what it would take to walk away and then imagine doing it. A bad deal is not worth it just to say you closed one, and walking away is rarely as bad as it sounds.

This mind-set will give you great psychological leverage when it comes time to negotiate.

Principle #4
Play the reluctant party

In most negotiations I've been involved in one party is more eager than the other — which in turn makes the other party more reluctant.

Which side would you rather be on?

Clearly you won't want to come across as the eager party, even though deep down inside you may be, because by taking on the role of the less eager party you are actually forcing the other party to take on the role of the eager party. So here are a few tricks you can use:

1. Use your body language to communicate your hesitancy.
While an enthusiastic negotiator will come across as tense, speak fast and often lean forward ready to leap forward, a reluctant negotiator will lean back, keep the tension in their bodies low, speak slowly and softly and slow down the pace of the negotiation.

2. Use the right language to show your indifference.
Reluctant parties in a negotiation *would* say things like, 'I don't know if we could actually do that', 'I'm not sure how you expect me to pay that price' or 'Would it work for you if we could do xxx?' They also ask a lot of questions and pose a lot of challenges.

They never show excitement — be relaxed and act 'cool'.

Principle #5
Negotiation is always about give and take

Some people may be tempted to use the information in this book to pressure others to do what they want. But that is not negotiation, more of a form of bullying.

It's important to understand the difference between influence and pressure as they are two very different beasts.

In negotiation, it's about the back and forth deal-making between two people.

You have to be prepared to give a little. In fact, it makes sense to prepare something in advance to trade, since it's perfectly fine to give something up that is of no consequence to you, but it should always come with a concession on the other party's end.

That's what smart negotiators do. They present a list of requests to the other party including some items that are really not that important to them, but by conceding these items during the negotiating process, they gain concessions from the other party.

The golden rule in trading concessions is never give a concession that is perceived to be greater in value than the one you just received. Only trade concessions that are equal in perceived value.

That's why it's called a negotiation, and it's a two-way street.

Of course, your job in any negotiation is to walk away with the best deal possible. It could be asking for a pay rise or making sure you get the best price on an appliance. But most people, unless they're not actively invested in what they're negotiating, will want to feel that they come out on top in some way. That they got a good deal.

Which means your job is also to help them feel that way. You do this by asking for something that you can later give up as part of the negotiation or setting your price high enough so that you have wriggle room to lower your asking price.

Simply asking for what you want outright, and not budging an inch, isn't likely to work.

Principle #6
Whenever you make a concession, make sure you get something in return.

Never make a concession in a negotiation without getting something in return. Your aim is to stop the other side from continuously asking for more and to clearly establish that every time they ask you for something you're going to expect a concession in return. What you're doing is conditioning the other side to always expect that they'll have to give you something in order to get a concession from you.

A 'concession' is just a fancy word for any time in a negotiation we give the other side something they want that you did not previously include in your offer or counteroffer. It may be more money, lower price, a longer term of settlement, a lower interest rate or anything else that helps get the deal done.

And as I said, wherever possible, you should negotiate 'something for something', a technique that children learn early on. Here's a good example of this:

Mother: 'I want you to tidy your room this morning.'

Son: 'Arrgh! OK, if I tidy my room can we go to the park this afternoon?'

Applying the 'something for something' principle helps to strengthen and maintain an overall negotiation position. However, this doesn't always you get what you ask for. For example, the mother could simply have said no or made a counteroffer of a smaller concession: 'No we can't go to the park today but perhaps we will all go tomorrow.'

Power negotiators slowly shrink the concessions they make as the negotiation process proceeds. They do this understanding that the pattern with which they make their concessions should subconsciously train the other party as to what to expect if they hold out for more. They always shrink the units of concession they make so that it feels to the other party that if they hold out for more they are only going to get less and less.

Some further thoughts on concessions:

- *Keep asking until they say no.* It is easy to feel you might cause offence if continually asking for concessions, but in most cases you have nothing to lose and may well end up with more than you anticipated.
- *Put a value to every concession.* When giving a concession, emphasise its value so the other party feels they are receiving something significant. Keep score of all concessions and use this to summarise how much you've given in as a means to resist further requests for concessions from them.

- *Slow and steady.* Make sure you don't give concessions too quickly or too early in the negotiation. This makes you seem too eager, which can raise the other party's expectations unnecessarily. Speed is an important signal to the other party of how keen you are to make a deal. Don't let your excitement get the better of you; keep your cool until the time is right.

Principle #7
Make the first offer

Back in the day, salesmen used to swear by the power of staying silent. Let the other person make the first offer, get them to decide where the value lies and then negotiate down (or up) from there.

This approach has gradually fallen out of favour as skilled negotiators realise what a risky strategy this is. If you allow someone else to determine the value, you're at the mercy of their judgment. You are letting them decide where the ballpark is, and that is very strong opening gambit that you're giving them!

What you want to do is mention price — the negotiating range — as soon as possible. You must be the one to set the value of the product or service in the other person's mind.

Because as I have discussed previously, value is such a relative term. No one, deep down, knows how much something is worth and they often need to be told a product's value through other people and what they pay.

The term that skilled negotiators use for making the first offer is 'anchoring the price'. Remember when I mentioned anchoring bias in a previous chapter? It sets the parameters for the negotiation to follow, and lets the other party know where the value is.

Remember anchoring is based on how human beings think and respond, and it is proven to work.

In a series of negotiation technique studies, researchers from Duke University, the University of Michigan, and the University of Houston found some interesting results when it came to anchoring price.

The researchers asked MBA students to negotiate a single-issue price deal and recorded who made the first offer, the amount of the offer, and the final deal outcome.

Interestingly, the negotiators who made the first offer felt more anxiety than those who did not — and, as a result, were less satisfied with their outcomes.

Yet, backing up prior bargaining studies, those who made first offers did better financially than those who did not.

The upshot is that while the negotiation process may *feel* tough, it was the most financially rewarding. Now, anchoring may not be for you. You may have a relationship with someone that you want to build over time, so one or two deals are not as important as the rewards of the sum of that relationship.

But in most situations, anchoring is devastatingly effective, especially when negotiating a price for big-ticket items, such as a property.

How to drop the anchor properly

Of course, anchoring the price is much more complicated than simply stating what you would like the final outcome to realistically be.

Adam D. Galinsky, who studies negotiation strategies at Northwestern University's Kellogg Graduate School of Management, points out that the first offer needs to be aggressive.

Aim high, and don't build in any concessions or compromises. This anchor figure should be one that you would be over the moon to achieve: don't make it ridiculous but be very ambitious.

Galinsky also makes a very wise point when it comes to the actual figsure you use. Now most people offer round numbers. They think it is easy on them and easier on the other party.

But here's what I do: I make very detailed offers, right down to the cents sometimes.

Just say that I am buying an apartment. I decide to make an opening offer around the $550,000 mark. Now there are good reasons why I have chosen that figure but going in at $550,000 looks like I plucked it out of the air.

So I offer $548,550. It's very specific and it speaks volumes about the research I have done. I usually accompany that offer, with a statement like, 'After factoring in the work that needs to be done on the property, I am willing to make the following offer...'

I see anchoring at work time and time again, and it is extremely effective. Much better to decide the ballpark figure than to be bamboozled by someone else's idea of how much something should cost.

Anchoring is a fantastic tool but be aware of the right time to use it. It works best in straight negotiations over price, where you can be as specific as possible. It may not work as effectively, for example, when you are negotiating time or a service, although you can still use the anchoring principle to set expectations.

In multi-issue negotiations, be aware that you may find it harder to drop the one anchor price as you are dealing with a number of different issues, albeit with the one person. This does not mean it's impossible, but you will have to stay on your toes.

Establish individual anchor points for each issue and offer a number of anchors at the one time. The person's reaction to each anchor can be a guide as to where their hard line is and what they prioritise, and it makes you look flexible.

Anchoring is also most effective when you are armed with all of the knowledge pertaining to a deal. This allows you to be bold but not too bold when anchoring the price. However, if you don't have a sense of 'market' value (what others have paid previously) and the details of the deal, it will be very hard to determine where to drop your anchor let alone whether or not you have achieved a solid deal.

Like any negotiation technique discussed in this book, it is only as good as the knowledge and the skills of the person behind it.

Principle #8
Strive to be innocent

To Power Negotiators, smart is dumb and dumb is smart. When you are negotiating, you're better off acting as if you know less than everybody else does, not more.

Have you ever noticed that as soon as people admit they really don't understand something, a lot of people rush in to help them out? If you are willing to let the other party feel smarter than you and feel in control in the exchange, you're likely to put yourself in the position of winning the negotiation.

I don't know about you, but I'm prepared to let my ego fall by the wayside when it comes to negotiations if it helps me make real dollars instead of psychological dollars.

Think about it — who would you rather do a deal with? Someone you felt more intelligent than, or someone who you suspected was smarter than you? I'm guessing the little voice inside your head is saying 'someone who's not smarter than me!'

Why? Because when you're negotiating with someone who may intimidate you a little — someone who you may feel is smarter or stronger or in a better negotiating position than you, are you comfortable or do you find yourself more on the defensive? And that defensive feeling doesn't put you in the position of power in the negotiation.

When you act dumb you'll often find others smile, thinking they have this pigeon just where they want him, and take him under their wing and help him out. Of course that's usually just when you have them where you want them. They often reveal more than they care to about their own needs and what they are willing to concede.

The problem is that most of us are too eager to show off just what we know. This can work against us. We can often reveal too much too soon about what we are willing to give up to get the deal.

We must let go of our ego satisfying position of 'know it all' and instead assume the profit-making position of innocence.

Do you remember the TV show *Columbo*? It was one of my favourites when I grew up. Peter Falk played a detective who walked around in an old raincoat and a mental fog, chewing on an old cigar butt. He constantly wore an expression that suggested he had just misplaced something and couldn't remember what it was, let alone where he had left it.

In fact, his success was directly attributable to how smart he was-by acting dumb. His demeanour was so disarming that the murderers came close to wanting him to solve his cases because he appeared to be so helpless.

The reason for acting innocent is that it diffuses the competitive spirit of the other side. How can you fight with someone who is asking you to help them negotiate with you?

How can you carry on any type of competitive banter with a person who says, 'I don't know, what do you think?' Most people, when faced with this situation, feel sorry for the other person and go out of their way to help him or her.

This concept is particularly useful when you're buying a product or service so here are five ways you can 'play dumb', just in case you need a little help with this:

1. *Ask plenty of questions.* Try saying something like 'I don't know...I'm new to this, you're the experts, so you're going

to have to help me out understanding this.' Let the seller tell you the facts and figures.

2. *Never, ever try to impress* the seller with displays of fancy terminology and general 'know-it-all-ness'.

3. If you do need to inject a fact into the discussion, try using *language* like 'If I remember this correctly, I've heard that if I make the full payment up front, rather than over 12 months, there is a substantial discount available' or 'I was talking with this real estate agent the other day and he told me that it's customary for the seller to pay for the building and pest inspection'.

4. *Talk slow and pause a lot.*

5. Make sure you do any number crunching slowly and step by step. Use paper, pencil or a calculator, rather than running numbers in your head.

Principle #9
The Flinch

Making the first offer is usually considered to be an advantage in negotiations but responding to a first offer with a measured 'flinch' can be just as effective in leading to an eventual negotiation win.

A flinch is a visible reaction when you hear the other party's opening offer — a show of shock, disgust or disbelief, even if you're happy with it, and the flinch works whether you are the buyer or the seller.

Here's how it works.

Imagine John goes into a camera store to buy the latest mirrorless DSLR camera. After being given a demonstration John asks the sales assistant the cost of the latest Nikon XYZ model.

The salesman says $1,500. No visible reaction from John, so the salesman adds *'And it's an extra $350 for this wide-angle lens'*. He watches his victim carefully. Still no reaction so he goes on, *'And with the special filters to put on the lens you cut out all the glare and protect the value of your camera these only cost extra $50.'*

John really wants this camera and walks out with his new toy.

Fifteen minutes later Jill walks into the same store and asked for a demonstration of the same camera. She likes it too, so asks how much it costs. The salesman replies $1,500. Jill who understands the power of good flinch, is visibly aghast and clasps her hands together and says *'$1,500! That's a lot of money for a camera.'*

The salesman wants to make a sale, so he quickly adds, *'And you need this wide-angle lens to be able to take all the photos of your vacation. While it normally costs $350, if you buy this camera today I'll throw it in for $250.'*

Jill is on a roll. Mouth wide open in astonishment she says *'$250 for another lens. I assumed it came as one package. You mean you charge extra for this lens!'*

The salesman now has had the tables turn on him so says, *'I'll throw in these extra special filters to put on your lens — they normally cost $50. Would you be happy with that?'*

Jill still looks a little concerned but agrees to this price and gets her camera considerably cheaper than John did.

Don't underestimate the power of a good flinch and don't be scared to try it. It's simply just another way of using Body Language to your advantage.

Remember…negotiating is a game and one of the rules of my game says that flinching is OK because it will achieve two objectives:

1. Getting the most value for the negotiator, and
2. Leaving your counterpart in the negotiations feeling that he or she did well.

Principle #10
Watch out for the Nibble

A common negotiating tactic used on salespeople is called 'nibbling'. Just as a mouse might nibble at a piece of cheese with small bites until it's completely gone, 'nibbling' is asking for small items, one at a time, and getting agreement on each until you've gotten a lot more than the other party bargained for.

Nibbling can be particularly effective near the end of a negotiation, when the other party is eager to reach a final agreement having invested a lot of time in the negotiation. You're more likely to gain on your nibbles after they've been worn down and just want to get a deal done.

The nibble works because it is small compared to the total deal and therefore seems insignificant. You might say, 'Oh, there is just one more thing — would it be possible...'

On the other hand, if someone is using the nibble on you then you should always ask for something in return. If they keep nibbling, ask for even bigger concessions in return. That should stop them.

Another way of countering this tactic is at the start of the negotiation, to lay out every issue you want to discuss, and ask your counterpart to do the same. Throughout the talks, continuously ask if there is anything else they want to put on the table. If they don't, you have given them every opportunity and should feel no guilt in turning down the nibble. If they attempt the nibble, have a set of small issues yourself that you can counter with. They will either accept or more likely back down and agree to the original deal as discussed.

Principle #11
Get comfortable with silence

We've all been in a situation involving an awkward silence. You know, one of those moments where you want to say some something, say anything, just to make it stop.

It's tough to keep quiet during those awkward silent moments, especially during a negotiation. Yet it's a vital skill for you to learn.

First let's talk about the why.

I've found that in many cases the party you are negotiating with will pause just before they make a big concession. But it's in this pause that many negotiators lose their advantage, because they rush to fill the void with words — sometimes to the point where they lose the concession!

Don't let this be you. Instead, learn to recognise that a meaningful, awkward quiet moment is a powerful tool to move you closer to the deal you want. It can also pry loose a critical piece of information. Remember, you are not alone in hating the discomfort of silence. The other party hates it too. But as a Power Negotiator you must learn to become comfortable with silence.

Often all you need is to bite your tongue for between five and 10 seconds, and the other party will blurt something out.

And yes, that 5–10 seconds will feel like forever, but here are four times it will benefit you to be silent:

1. Right after you ask for a concession.
2. Right after you have flinched and said something like: 'That's a lot of money you're asking.'
3. Right after you've asked them a tough question.
4. When you've just been offered a great deal. Even though you want to rush in and hug them, don't. Be silent for a moment to let them stew and doubt before you accept.

Principle #12
Know when to talk, but also know when to be silent

I've just explained that one of the secret weapons of good negotiators is to ask questions and then remain silent.

The person asking the questions controls the conversation. And you're not always asking just to find out information, because if you have done your homework before commencing the negotiation, you should already know many of the answers.

You've probably read that lawyers are taught to never ask a question without already knowing the answer. That's also good advice for negotiators.

What you are really doing is getting the other person to talk, perhaps to verify your information, but really to feel more comfortable working with you, and to build rapport.

OK, let's put the shoe on the other foot — when you are asked a question as part of a negotiation, there is no rule that says you have to answer. Try remaining silent.

What usually happens is that the questioner will start talking again because amateurs talk too much while professionals use silence.

Another trick is to throw the question back by say something like 'Before I answer that, please tell me why you asked that question.'

The reason I suggested remaining silent is because silence makes most of us feel uncomfortable. In today's world we are conditioned to noise, not to being silent.

Next time you are negotiating, try this little trick…

When the other party says something like 'Well, that's my offer', don't say a word for 10 seconds. To inexperienced negotiators 10 seconds will seem like an eternity.

It's practically guaranteed they will jump in with another offer or more information, anything to break the silence.

Another good trick is to learn to pause for a second or two between sentences — especially if you're a fast talker.

It helps the other party take in what you've just said and analyse it.

Just like a good comedian understands the importance of timing and pauses, a good negotiator understands the art of pausing between sentences for more emphasis.

Principle #13
People want the path of least resistance

OK, this may sound a little harsh, but most people are a little lazy and have no interest in expending unnecessary effort. If you gave someone the option of the easy route or the hard route and the destination was the same, what would they choose?

It's human nature. We're hard-wired to do what is required and no more. There is nothing wrong with that, especially as we are all so busy these days, most people struggle to get the bare minimum done.

Very few people enjoy the cut-and-thrust of a volatile negotiation. North Korean dictators notwithstanding, it's fair to say most people are consensus-seeking and would rather avoid a fight. This means it's up to you to ensure you don't come across as aggressive or demanding when trying to secure what you want.

As soon as someone senses hostility or strong emotion, they'll close up and shut down. This spells the end of the negotiation and you should ensure the experience is as pleasant for the other person as possible.

Difficult people don't get the best deals — easy people do. So, as a negotiator, you should recognise that most people will choose the path of least resistance. They will be attracted to businesses or people who make it easy for them to say yes and move forward with a chosen course and this who remove obstacles along the way.

Use this knowledge wisely.

Principle #14
Negotiation isn't about defeating someone else

Many people confuse negotiation with 'defeating their opponent' and because of the cynical approach they take it often ends with no one being happy!

My advice is to always put your competitive nature to one side when negotiating. Don't try and 'crush' the opposition as your ego will just end up ruining it.

Similarly separate the other party from the issues you're negotiating. This means you can negotiate hard, but you should never be hard on the other person. Don't be rude. Don't insult them, threaten them or be unfriendly.

To be persuasive you need to put yourself in the other party's position. You need to understand their needs, how they're feeling about the situation and what they'd like to achieve.

This way you're more likely to be able to construct a deal that will persuade them.

Principle #15
Slow and steady wins the race

In all my time of taking part in negotiations and watching others attempt to close deals, I have learned how to pick the best negotiator at the table in the first few seconds.

Want to know how to spot them? They take their time and they're not in a rush. They may speak a lot or very little, but there will be still be a sense that they have all day.

Of course they don't, but they're wonderful at giving the impression that they will stick at this deal until they're satisfied.

Principle #16
The most important word in negotiations

The little two letter word 'if' is a very powerful negotiation tool. 'If I can do this, will you do that?' Or 'If you can do this, I'll definitely do that.'

For example:

- 'If you can double your order then I can certainly meet your price.'
- 'If you can pay my price I can arrange for delivery by the weekend.'
- 'If I can convince my manager that your offer is not an issue pricewise, will you be able to sign the contract today?'

Principle #17
Negotiate with the decision maker

I've seen many inexperienced negotiators work too hard on a deal, often spread out over days or weeks, eventually meeting all the other party's needs and then get told 'Well that looks good, now I have to clear it with my manager.'

It doesn't matter whether you're buying or selling, always negotiate with the decision maker.

How do you know who the decision maker is? Just ask. A polite way of asking without offending the other party is, 'Other than you, who will be involved in making the final decision?'

Principle #18
Keep your cool

If the other party starts talking more loudly, it's likely that they mistakenly believe you'll listen more attentively.

Now it would be instinctive to raise your voice and talk back loudly, but a clever technique is to pause and talk back softly. Firstly, it is likely you'll make the loud talker feel a little uncomfortable and it will make them listen more carefully than if you spoke in a loud voice.

That's better than the alternative of speaking loudly, which may just turn the negotiation into an argument.

Principle #19
Never assume the other party believes you

Negotiating expert Roger Dawson teaches that you should never assume that people believe you.

Now don't be offended by people's natural reluctance to believe you. Remember we live in a world where we are continually bombarded with marketing messages. We can't possibly believe all of them.

The cornerstone to your ability to persuade others or complete a successful negotiation will rest on your level of credibility (remember Dr Cialdini's Principle of Authority?) So while power persuaders learn to build credibility into their sales presentations or negotiation discussions, they have already built a level of authority through their social media presence and their marketing initiatives.

Another way to build credibility is by pointing out little flaws or disadvantages as you present an argument for your product or service.

Dawson also teaches to never assume that people understand you.

The problem is the other party is probably too embarrassed to tell you that you've lost them. People don't like to admit that something is too complicated for them to understand. However, a confused mind will always say 'no'.

Principle #20
Agree on the big picture

I've found that if both parties want a deal to proceed, they won't let the details get in the way. But if they don't really want it to proceed, negotiating all the fine details usually won't clinch the deal.

This means sometimes it is useful to get an agreement on the principle first and then go back and hammer out the details. This seems to work better than getting bogged down in details that get in the way of the final deal.

Principle #21
It's never over...

When the other party says, 'That's it…take it or leave it!' ignore what they're saying and start using 'What ifs'. This goes back to making a bigger pie like I discussed at the beginning of this book.

'What if I could persuade my management to allow you to pay over 90 days?' Or 'What if I threw in a year's free servicing?'

Now you won't always reach an agreement straight away, meaning at times you may walk away from a particular deal and feel that you could have asked for more. Just because the 'formal' part of the negotiation is over, doesn't mean you can't find a way to ensure your wishes are met.

Continue to negotiate until you're satisfied. Analyse what went wrong and try a different approach. Put your wishes back on the table, later down the track or when you have something else to offer in return.

Principle #22
In negotiation, nothing is off limits

Sometimes when we enter negotiations, we limit ourselves by what we think we can and can't ask for. It happens all the time. We either think the price is set or 'it's just not the done thing' to ask for a perk or an upgrade.

Australians, in particular, suffer from this mindset: the idea that certain things are not up for negotiation. But they are.

One of the laws of negotiation is that everything is on the table. Now, what you put on the table may not be agreed to, but it's worth putting it up for negotiation regardless.

Nothing is off limits; everything is up for negotiation.

Principle #23
You can't wing it

You may be the most charming person on earth. Doors may open for you, people may want to be around you, but nothing will out-smart old-fashioned research.

If you walk into a serious negotiation and think you can rely solely on charm, then you're mistaken. The person who has done the most research is the person in any negotiating session that is likely to come out satisfied.

You may be able to wing it a couple of times, but eventually your luck will run out. Remember: knowledge and preparation is power.

Principle #24
Never believe anyone else is entirely on your side

Trust yourself; you have your own interests entirely at heart.

As a buyer, would you go up to a seller, show your bank

preapproval letter, explain how desperate you are to buy their property, then ask the them to tell you what you should offer?

If you are a seller, would you tell a potential buyer your absolute bottom line?

No sane person would do such things, yet every day buyers allow others to make decisions for them. These others could be a real estate agent, a car salesman, a relative or even a friend.

Yes, you certainly want to ask others for advice, but my point is that while these people may not consciously deceive or purposely lead you astray; everybody's interests are different, each has their own goals and yours are always going to be different and sometimes conflict with mine.

Principle #25
The person with the greater power will get the better deal

This principle is so important that I've devoted the whole of the next chapter to it, but in short no one will negotiate with you unless they feel you have the power to help them or hurt them in some way.

Of course this power can be can be real or perceived. Often you have more power than you know, and the other party has less power than they appear to have.

You must be clear about both to maximise your success in negotiating.

You must have something the other person wants, or you must be able to withhold something he wants for the other person to take the negotiations seriously. You may have a product or service or as a customer you'll have the money to pay for that product or service that the other party wants. Either way it's important to see the negotiation from the other's point of view so that you can position yourself for the maximum benefit to yourself.

Principle #26
Understand the power of the 'Decoy Effect'

Once you become aware of the Decoy Effect, you'll start to see this tactic everywhere and you'll be able to put it to good use yourself. Marketers and salespeople have been using it for years because when it comes to forcing the hand of the buyer, there is no pricing strategy that comes close.

So what is it?

The Decoy Effect is the phenomenon where consumers swap their preference between two options when presented with a third option.

The Decoy Effect was a term first coined by academics Joel Huber, John Payne and Christopher Puto in 1981, and it has been relied on by companies to sell consumer goods ever since. These academics conducted a number of experiments in which university students were asked to choose between two different models of consumer goods, including cars, restaurants, films and TVs. When students were given a third option — the decoy designed to nudge them toward picking a certain option— the strategy worked in directing them to the target option.

This is very powerful stuff because most of us like our decisions to be obvious ones.

By that I mean we like to see a clear and obvious choice so we have no regrets or worries about buying the wrong thing. We're often overwhelmed by choice these days. Compared to when I was growing up, today we have a stack of choice among any number of products and it's easy to get over-whelmed simply buying cheese or a loaf of bread! There are so many brands and types available, and many of us will be hit with 'decision fatigue' when trying to decide what type to buy.

What the Decoy Effect proves is that we don't want an exten-sive set of criteria when shopping. Instead we will base our choice on the best value and on what is available rather than on any absolute preference. This means people are highly susceptible to being 'nudged' towards a certain product choice based on value for money.

Let's see how the decoy effect works in real life, which is really the best way to truly understand how powerful it is.

Let's pretend you are wanting to purchase a set of headphones.

Headphone A has inferior technology but is only $39. Tempting.

Headphone B, however, has improved technology with better sound but is also more expensive at $89.

In order to direct the consumer to the $89 purchase, marketers and sellers will use a decoy product, Headphone C, priced to make Headphone B look even more attractive. It costs $89, so it's the same price, but it lacks the impressive sound technology.

Which one would you opt for?

Gary Mortimer, Associate Professor in Marketing and Consumer Behaviour at the Queensland University of Technology, used a great example of the decoy effect in action when looking at subscription offers for *The Australian* newspaper. As Mortimer pointed out in his essay on The Conversation website, the newspaper used a classic decoy model to push readers towards the target offer.

Essentially, readers were offered three options: digital (50 cents a day), digital and the weekend paper (50 cents a day) and digital plus six-day paper for $1 a day.

Now, why on Earth would anyone choose the digital-only option when the digital plus weekend paper costs exactly the same amount? So in this case, the digital-only subscription is the decoy to draw readers to the digital and weekend paper option, which is the most profitable option for the company.

Although subscribers pay more to access the six-day paper, it's very expensive to print newspaper and many media companies are pushing the digital and weekend paper only option.

Another great example involves popcorn and *National Geographic*, believe it or not!

The magazine ran an experiment to test how the decoy effect influences consumers to buy a large popcorn rather than a small or medium one. As part of the experiment, consumers were offered a small bucket of popcorn for $3 or a large one for $7.

Most people opted for the cheaper option, until the option of a third was presented to them: a medium popcorn that was smaller than the large, but only cost 50 cents less at $6.50.

Most could see that they got better value for money when buying the $7 bucket, so that is the one they went with. The fact that they may not have been that hungry and were only after a small popcorn to begin with is irrelevant. It became about value, and once the decoy was introduced — the medium popcorn — it made the $7 value option the obvious choice.

What is most interesting about the Decoy Effect is the way it highlights human behaviour and patterns. When it comes to making decisions, we all follow some pretty obvious patterns and are not as unique as we may have thought. By using a decoy item, you can direct your prospect to the 'best option available' which is, of course, your preferred option.

This is great news for you, the negotiator.

By learning the power of certain proven marketing principles, such as the Decoy Effect, you'll be able to use them to steer people in the direction you wish them to go in — without any pushy sales tactics or sales mumbo jumbo.

Principle #27
Use the Power of Stories

Want to hear the story? Often when you hear this question you suddenly pay attention to the person telling the story. Everybody love stories, don't they?

That's why storytelling is one of the most powerful covert persuasive techniques you can use to influence people. Storytelling is a technique I use all the time to help influence others by getting under their radar.

When you tell a story you lower the other party's resistance, make complicated things easier to understand and invoke the other persons emotions. When you tell a story you give your prospect the ability to temporarily escape the real world and enter another dimension. When they're in storyland their minds are open to accept concepts and ideas they may have otherwise rejected.

You will find many online marketers employ stories instead of directly selling their products and services. I'm sure you've seen those rags to riches stories, haven't you? They tell you how the other person started out broke, homeless and depressed then they found the secret formula that enabled them to achieve all their dreams and now they are ready to share their secrets with you.

Marketers cleverly used these storytelling techniques rather than directly telling you to buy their products and services. They recognise that storytelling can touch hearts, change moods and alter emotions. They know that readers will feel involved in the story and would like to attain the same happy ending as the person in the story.

The lesson for you is that when telling stories as a persuasion technique, engage as many of your prospect's senses as possible. Let them see, hear, smell, taste and feel various aspects of your story.

Practice this and you will find that storytelling becomes one of your most effective covert persuasion techniques in your arsenal.

Principle #28
People don't only buy because of price

It's a big mistake I think the people only buy on price. If that was the case people wouldn't buy Mercedes or Bentley's – they would only buy Suzuki cars.

However it's normal for customers to ask "What's your best price?"

The price question comes down to:

1. Are you going to delivering value to your customer?
2. Can they afford you?

In other words, is it expensive from a value point of view, or an affordability point of view?

So before getting caught in the price conversation with your prospect they have to understand how you will add value and this is most likely in one or more of the following three ways:
1. You'll fix a problem they have
2. You'll prevent them from making mistakes or losing money etc. or…
3. You'll improve their situation

When asked about price my standard answer is something like: *"What's more important to you – price or cost?"*

The customer won't usually understand what you mean and won't know how to respond.

In fact, here's how a conversation could go with a prospect for our Property Strategists at Metropole – where I believe we add a lot of value – when we build our clients a strategic Property Plan at "the cost" of $3,995, but a customer queries the price.

"When it comes to helping you plan for your future financial freedom the price of our Strategic Property Plan is $3,995 plus GST.

"And I'm interested to know, on a scale of 1 to 10, where 10 is expensive, what is your immediate reaction to/perception about that price?"

Whatever the client responds, we thank them for their honesty and continue.
"Let me ask you, what's more important to you – price or cost?"

The client is not sure what we mean, so we explain…

"Let's look at the difference between price and cost.

"Cost is the $3,995 you invest to get the typical $25,000 better capital growth each year our clients achieve by just outperforming the market by 2% clients.

"Now over 10 years that's a quarter of a million dollars in extra value that we know our clients get from implementing our Strategic Plan.

"That's a huge return on investment – I'm not even sure I can calculate it.

"Of course I'm not talking about the absolute capital growth on their investments – I'm talking about the extra capital growth by only are performing the market a small amount and obviously many of our clients achieve much, much better return than that.

"So on that same scale, how would you rate the cost of $3,995 to access value of $250,000 extra return?"

They will usually rate lower than their first rating for price.

"So the difference between price and cost relates to what you get from the spend, rather than the spend itself... is that fair?"

The client will typically agree.

"Great, thank you. So this is all about the ROI, but you know, there is another cost isn't there..."

Again the client won't know how to respond.

"If you don't get that quarter of a million dollars in value, if

you don't take action to make that happen, there is a cost of inaction. There is a quarter of a million dollars cost of not doing it."

"In fact there's another cost – the cost of all the mistakes investors make – that we help prevent because we've been there and done that and know all the landmines. Particularly in today's more complex markets."

"And I just wonder, which cost are you happiest to invest in, the cost of return or the cost of inaction?"

Remember: life is one big negotiation.

While many people think of negotiation as a set activity with defined parameters, it is nothing of the sort. We negotiate in subtle ways every day: for the best table at a restaurant, for the best car deal, for control of the remote.

Life is one big bargaining event, and if you become very good at negotiating it can really make a difference to the quality of your life.

14 SOURCES OF POWER IN A NEGOTIATION

■ ■ ■

Every time you negotiate you'll either have the feeling of being in control or not, of being comfortable or uncomfortable. You may feel like you've got the upper hand, or you may feel intimidated.

What controls these feelings of having power? Why do they swing from one party to the other during the negotiations?

Well…all power is based on perception. If you think you've got it, then you've got it. If you don't think you have it, even if you do have it, you won't really have it.

Truth is, there are many types of power and realising that you have much more power than you think is crucial to using it effectively. Again, like all the other techniques you're learning in this book, you can use your persuasive powers to create positive outcomes or to take advantage of the other party. By now you know that while the choice is yours, there's really only one way to win in the long term and that's to use your power negotiation skills to help others get what they need.

The late Wayne Berry, who was a good friend, has done some excellent work in this field and I will spend some time now outlining Wayne's concept of the sources of power in a negotiation, adding a few of my own. So, let's look at where this power comes from.

1. ATTITUDE POWER

If you think you've got power, you've got power. Power is a state of mind, so your attitude going into any negotiation speaks volumes about how successful you're likely to be. Feeling meek and mild, not sure of your own offering? You're not likely to succeed.

If, however, you adopt an air of authority (not arrogance, as there is a difference) and remain calm and detached, then you're giving yourself a great chance at success.

A great attitude to adopt is 'Negotiating is just a game!' This attitude is very empowering because by maintaining a sense of detachment you are much more empowered then if you're emotionally involved. In other words, care…but not that much!

2. TIME POWER

Time, or lack of it, is an incredible source of power in negotiations, so understanding how time can give you power will really put you at a great advantage. Often a deadline will be set in negotiations but remember…this deadline was most likely arbitrarily set by another person, meaning deadlines are almost always flexible and can usually be extended.

So rather than falling into the trap of someone else's time power, understanding the concept that deadlines can be changed can be very empowering. Conversely, placing deadlines on others can empower you.

Real estate agents are masters at this. Why do you think the auction system is so successful? A group of people gather at the same place, at the same time, and bid over a property that will fall under the hammer within 15 minutes. If that is not time pressure (and scarcity), I don't know what is.

Cyber hackers use time pressure for their own evil purposes. Often when they hack into people's computers they will tell them that they have 15 minutes, or whatever their nominated period is, to respond before their computer is infected.

They then pose as a computer support service to 'help' the person ward off the cyber breach, which is doesn't even exist. By the time, the person realises this, they've paid the hackers and maybe even handed over their online passwords!

The idea is to create a kind of pressure vacuum in which the person is rushed into signing or agreeing to something before they can pull out or have time to think about the consequences.

A handy rule to remember about time power:

- High time pressure = low power
- Low time pressure = high power

Now another interesting aspect of time as a source of power in negotiations is that, as a rule, the more time invested, the more flexible a person is likely to become in the negotiations. Remember when I discussed Sunk Cost bias?

Let me explain with an example you're probably familiar with.

When buying a car you most likely have a rough idea of which model you'd like to purchase so you go to a dealer and the salesperson explains all the car's features to you, goes through all the options, takes you for a test drive and after an hour or so finally sits down with you and tries to nut out a deal.

But it's quite likely that you will give another dealer a call and ask him to better this first price.

As you can imagine, the first dealer is more likely to lower his price because of the amount of time and emotion he has invested in the negotiation, while to the second dealer you're just another voice over the phone looking for a bargain.

Remember this and use this ploy but watch out for experienced negotiators who use this tactic on you. Now I'm not saying don't invest time in negotiations, just be careful that you don't become too emotionally involved because of the time invested.

3. INFORMATION POWER

In negotiations the more information you have, generally the more power you possess.

Knowing more than the person you're negotiating with is very powerful, so before getting involved in a major negotiation do your homework carefully.

I use information power in my real estate negotiations all the time. That's because property is an imperfect market (where not everybody has the same amount of information). My knowledge, contacts and experience give me an edge over other less informed, more emotional parties.

In other types of negotiation, you may have to ask the other party for information. When you seek out information, don't believe everything you've been told and don't be scared to question its validity. In fact, it pays to act dumb. Sounding innocent and naïve is a great negotiating strategy and you're more likely to get answers to your questions than if you act smug and like a know it all.

You could ask questions like: 'What do you mean?' 'Could you please explain that?' 'Is that really the best you can do?'

4. EXPERT POWER

This is really similar to information power that we just discussed and is an example of Dr. Cialdini's Principle of Authority. An expert is an individual who has expertise that is highly valued, and this gives them a level of power regardless of their status.

You may have expert knowledge about technical, administrative or personal matters. The harder it is to replace your expertise the more expert power you have in the negotiation.

During a negotiation you can establish your expertise in the mind of the other party by:
- Quoting facts or figures
- Name dropping
- Referring to research or technical documents
- Becoming an influencer on social media or in the press.

5. COMMITMENT POWER

In all walks of life, those who are prepared to hang in there, to keep going when the going gets tough, often come out on top.

By sheer force of will and grit, they persevere and get what they want.

Which is why, in any negotiation, the person who wants it badly enough will often get what they want! They're the ones prepared to keep haggling until a better deal comes their way. They say no when they need to, which allows them to say yes to the right deal.

6. STRATEGY POWER

The negotiator with a plan or strategy is very empowered, compared to the negotiator who doesn't know which way is up.

Not only is it important to have a strategy, you must to stick to it. This can be difficult during negotiations where the stakes and emotions are high and you're thinking on your feet. It can also prove difficult if the other person is an especially skilled negotiator.

The trick is to keep calm. Don't lose your cool or go off course. Remember to keep your strategy in mind at all times.

If a curve ball is thrown your way, something that you weren't expecting, take a moment to absorb it and keep moving forward with your strategy at the front of your mind.

You may find that if you're new to negotiations you tend to veer off your strategy halfway through. Don't let this bother you too much as that is natural at first. But make sure you keep practising and soon sticking to your strategy will feel like second nature.

7. ALTERNATIVE OPTIONS POWER

The more options you have, the more power you possess. That makes sense doesn't it?

Before you head into a negotiation, take the time to look at all of your available options. Write them down to show yourself that the deal is not the be all and end all. If you find that you don't have any alternative options, it's your job to go and find some. It's that important, because if you walk into a negotiation without any alternatives then you're handing over all your power to the other person.

Now, during a negotiation the other party may say they have lots of other options but in reality they're just saying this to boost their own power and weaken yours. Don't be afraid to ask them about their alternatives. Really try and nail them down on the specifics.

If you do manage to trip them up or they're unable to detail the alternatives, you'll have pulled off a delicate power shift that works in your favour.

As a salesperson one way of removing this source of power from the other party is to make what you're offering unique in some way. For example, including something which only you can offer, like a particular service or access to some specialised knowledge, makes it very difficult for the other party to compare apples with apples.

8. WALK-AWAY POWER

If you have alternative options then naturally it will follow that you have the power to walk away.

Make sure you think about this and are fully prepared to walk away from the negotiation if things fall over. There is no point in having alternative options if you're not willing to use the power that comes from knowing you can walk away at any point.

Yet it's often our pride or ego that stops us from doing this. And if you're a competitive person, you may struggle to walk away from a negotiation, believing that if you just keep going, you'll lock in the deal. Sure this approach has some merit. As discussed, it takes a determined person who is prepared to 'hang in there' to secure a deal. But a bad deal is a bad deal.

Know when there is no point in persevering and walk away. Save your efforts for the deals that are worth it.

What if you walk away and the other party doesn't try and stop you, or doesn't come after you or call you in a couple of days to try and continue the negotiation?

Can you come back? Of course you can.

As long as you're armed with a logical reason the only thing that would stop you returning is your pride. Don't let pride stop you — remember it's only a game.

9. BRAVERY POWER

You've heard the saying 'no guts, no glory'? Well, that is especially true in negotiations where the bravest person, the one most willing to take a risk, often emerges triumphant.

That doesn't mean you need to be a risky person, just someone willing to take a risk when the time is right and your gut instinct tells you to go for it.

I've always found that the most successful people are those that are brave enough to take calculated risks. They don't take risks for the fun of it, you wouldn't call them adrenalin junkies. But they don't let fear stop them from taking a leap when the time is right.

10. LOCATION POWER

Doctors have a term for people who become visibly anxious in a doctor's surgery, it's called White Coat Syndrome. What this means is that some people can become so fearful of bad news when visiting a doctor that their blood pressure or heart rate shoots up.

This is a telling example of how the environment we're in can really influence how we feel, how relaxed we are and how well we negotiate.

For example, negotiating on the other party's 'home turf' can give them tremendous confidence and may make you feel intimidated. On the other hand, you may want the other party to feel relaxed and comfortable.

Car dealers understand the power that the environment creates. Have you noticed how many of them now have a café in the dealership, where you can sit in a relaxed, more familiar atmosphere sipping a latte rather than across the desk from a salesperson?

As a salesperson, how could you use this trick in your sales environment?

When negotiating it's important to choose a location that will bring out the best in you. It could be your boardroom or it could be a cafe. Think about how relaxed you are in various negotiating environments and always choose the one that suits you best.

11. STATUS POWER

Titles are an interesting source of power and status, especially in the corporate world. It's a reality of human nature that we're so easily impressed and even intimidated by titles or status!

But remember…titles are just a few letters before or after somebody's name. They're just a label, and often the qualities and powers that come with them are imagined unless you are the Prime Minister of Australia or the President of the USA. So on the one hand, don't be intimidated by other people's titles, but on the other hand, if you have an important-sounding title, don't be afraid to use that in a negotiation setting. Come to the negotiation with business cards and, if the timing is right, mention your role and its responsibilities.

Be aware, too, that titles may be used on you. The c-suite (CEO, COO, etc.) of any large company consists of a wide range of people, some of whom are very good at their jobs, while with others you may wonder, 'How did they get here?'

I learned a long time ago to take titles with a grain of salt. I've met PAs that would be better CEOs than their bosses, and I'm sure you've seen in your work life that talent doesn't always rise to the top.

So be respectful of a person with a significant title, but never be awed.

12. POPULARITY POWER

Most of the time, what you're negotiating will be something that is in-demand: your time, your money, your service or a product.

Knowing that other people, people outside the negotiation space, want what you're bargaining over will give you enormous power.

Let's say that your car insurer has raised the cost of your premium. You decide to negotiate a better deal by asking them to match a deal that you have secured through another insurer elsewhere.

Most insurers will try and match your quote, or better it, because they know that your business matters and you can always take it elsewhere.

Showing that you're prepared to move insurers if they don't match the competitor's offer is a display of your popularity power. Realising how much companies want your business, and acting on it, is very powerful.

13. REPUTATION POWER

The better your reputation in whatever field you work in, the more reputation power you have.

That's why it's so important to behave with respect towards other people at all times. People will remember how you made them feel, rather than how many billions of dollars of deals you closed in the past few years.

If you're successful and you treat people ethically and kindly, you'll gain a great reputation in your field.

This gives you the upper hand going into any negotiation because the other party already knows that you'll behave respectfully, which means you're more likely to have a successful negotiation and secure what you're after.

If, however, you have a reputation for doing wrong by people, it's possible the other party will already have his or her back up.

14. BRAIN POWER

It's important to pay as much attention to your overall brain health and wellbeing as it is to your negotiation strategies.

There will be times in any negotiation where you'll be forced to think on your feet. Someone will say or do something that surprises you and you'll need to be flexible enough in your thinking to know how to handle it.

If you're operating at peak brain function then this won't throw you off. If, however, you're tired or grumpy, then you may not react as well.

Ensure your brain power is at full capacity by getting enough sleep, exercising and eating healthily.

15. VOLATILE POWER

I can guarantee that, at least once in your life, you've dealt with someone who was excellent at using their volatile power.

They're the ones who blow their fuse, hit the roof, essentially create a disturbance — sometimes loudly and threateningly — when something doesn't go their way.

They may be quite weak-willed people, with small reserves of resilience, but they actually have quite a lot of power. Why? Because people are afraid of them. They become so volatile no one gives them much work and they're left to their own devices.

This is a power that you don't want to cultivate. Ever. It's a cheap way of gaining power and it only ends up with people avoiding you.

It's much better to gain power through others' respect for you!

As you can see, there really are so many factors that affect how much power you have, or are perceived to have, in a negotiation. Hopefully, the examples I have given above have broadened your understanding of the different power dynamics in a negotiation scenario.

Being aware of each of these types of power will help you leverage them to maximum effect in a negotiation, and you'll also be able to dilute their impact when you see them in other people.

And remember a large part of the power you'll have in a negotiation is perception and if you think you've got it you've got it. And if you don't think you've got it, you haven't.

As a negotiator you'll continually be confronted by objections, so in the next chapter we'll look at a seven step process to handle objections like a pro.

HANDLING OBJECTIONS

The first book I ever read on sales techniques was mainly focused on handling objections. Boy have things changed since then. Today smart salespeople and negotiators build rapport, understand their clients' needs, offer an appropriate solution and then have very few objections to handle because they're closing the gap between where the client is today and where they want to be — I've discussed this concept before.

However, as a negotiator or a salesperson you're likely to come up against objections all the time, so let's look at the best way of handling them.

Now I've already explained my two favourite techniques in the chapter on hypnotic language:
1. Feel, felt, found, and
2. Positive, positive, positive, negative.

These sound so simple but are powerful objection handling tools, but sometimes you need more, so let's break down objection handling into simple steps:

Step 1: Pause and slow down the pace

When I first started selling and an objection was raised my initial response would be to interrupt the customer and virtually pounce on them with the list of reasons why their objection was wrong, and I'm sure I would have been speaking much faster than normal.

Clearly this was the wrong way to do things but that's how most people handle objections.

Today when I hear an objection I pause, even longer than the typical pauses I insert into a sales or negotiation discussion when I'm trying to create effect. I slow things down to try and regain trust from my prospect rather than rile them because if I upset them, whatever follows won't matter.

Step 2: Clarify the objection with questions

I have found that the real objection is often misunderstood and sometimes the other party doesn't really tell you their true objection, so if you don't clarify them you may press the wrong issue.

Again, in my early days I would react with a knee-jerk, long, loud monologue.

Instead today I validate the prospect's concern and clarify their objection before answering.

The great tactic I learned from Chris Voss in his book *Never Split the Difference* is to repeat the last few words of your prospect's sentence. Voss suggests you do this with an upward voice tone (like you're asking a question) because this triggers the other party to elaborate.

This is really another form of mirroring that you learned in the section on NLP. You could say something like:
'The price is too high?'
'The timing isn't right for you?'
'This won't solve the problem?'

Then once again pause and you'll almost certainly find the other party will fill the silence with further explanation. In fact, you may have to use this mirroring technique a couple of times in a row to peel away the onion so you can you get to their true objection.

Never ask *'Why?'* when trying to clarify objections as it doesn't really clarify. It's more likely to be seen as threatening and questions the validity of the other party's objection, putting them on the defensive.

Instead you could ask why without actually saying the word:
'Can you help me understand what's causing that concern?'

Step 3: Validate the Objection

Rather than belittling the objection *validate* it — like you do using the Feel, Felt Found model. 'I understand how you *feel*

John, I have found many of our clients *felt* that way when they first heard (fill in the blank).'

You see…many people go through life feeling misunderstood, but if you're the person who understands them, you'll carry powerful influence.

You'll benefit by saying something like: *'That's a valid concern. It seems like you're (fill in the blank).'*

Fill in the blank with an *emotion* you observed the are other party expressing. If you can look past the objection to what they're feeling, you're showing the other party that you understand them.

'That's a valid concern Bill. It seems like you're are bit uncertain what to do here.'
'That's a valid concern Kate. It seems like you're worried you may end up paying too much.'
'That's a valid concern Dennis. It seems like you I'm worried you may be biting off more debt than you can chew.'

Step 4: Isolate the Objection

Some objections are smoke screens. The other party's words and what's actually stopping them from moving forward are often different.

It's your job to make sure you're addressing the true objection. Otherwise you're wasting your time because once you've handled the original objection, they just come up with another one. That's what I was getting at a moment ago when I suggested you should peel back the layers of the onion objections.

Here's a good phrase that should elicit the true objection: '*If we manage to solve that issue completely what are the obstacles we would have to overcome before moving forward?*'

If the other party voices *other* objections, chances are those are the real things you need to overcome. And if they don't have any others then the first objection mentioned is the right one. Well done…you've isolated the objection.

Step 5: Ask for Permission

Now it's time to get the other party to look at things differently — your way. This is when some of the hypnotic words and phrases we've discussed earlier can be used. But before you do, you need to make the other party receptive to a different way of thinking.

I always as for permission to make some suggestions. But I don't say: '*Can I make some suggestions?*' because this can trigger defensiveness and the other person may will not be receptive to your suggestions. They're likely to smile, nod and then ignore everything you say.

If you've got teenagers, you'll know what I mean.

Here's the phrase that I find works well: *'Can I bounce a few thoughts off of you?'*

This question implies that you, not the other party, are the vulnerable one and doesn't sound as commanding.

Step 6: Reframe the objection

One of the most important parts a negotiation or any sales process is maintaining a positive vibe in the face of objection. And one of the best skills to achieve this is reframing.

Objection reframing is the process of taking the objection and turning the situation into a positive in the mind of the other person. When people feel positive about a situation, they are more open to making a change or making a purchase.

The best negotiators use this instinctively to help them solve problems and overcome objections. They approach conflicts as opportunities, not deal-breakers. They look at ways to fix things, rather than fixate on the conflicts themselves.
When you receive an objection reframe it as something other than a 'no' so you can continue with your negotiation.

- Reframe the objection as a misunderstanding (and take the blame for this yourself).
- Reframe the objection by taking the subject and turning it around.
- Reframe a small difference as being the critical difference.
- Reframe 'required specific experience' to 'relevant experience'.

For example:

- *I can see that this is not making sense. Sorry — let me put it another way.*
- *Yes, red is an unusual colour. It will make you look really original.*
- *The cost may be high, but the cost of inaction may be higher.*

Reframing uses what the other person has given you, which makes it more difficult for them to deny it. For example, you can reframe:

- A problem as an opportunity
- A weakness as a strength
- An impossibility as a distant possibility
- A distant possibility as a near possibility
- Oppression ('against me') as neutral ('doesn't care about me')
- Unkindness as lack of understanding

For example:

- *You say it can't be done in time. But what if we staged delivery or got in extra help? I'm sure we can produce an acceptable product in the timeframe.*
- *It's not so much doing away with old ways as building a new and exciting future.*
- *We have shown we can argue well. Maybe this means we can also agree well.*

Reframing is a challenging skill, but luckily, it is also a learnable skill. Practice it and you will have another great tool in your toolbox to use when you work with your clients.

Step 7: Confirm the resolution

Now this step is important — you want to come to a resolution and finalise a deal so don't lead the other party to say what you want to hear. This leaves the objection unresolved, killing your deal later on.

Instead say: *'What part of your concern do you feel is left unaddressed?'*

This will allow the other party to air any further concerns and if they don't — congratulations, you've overcome their objection.

In isolation each of these steps seem simple. But when you put all seven together, magic can happen.

SECTION THREE:

PUTTING IT INTO PRACTICE

I n this section I'm going to share ideas for how to use the concepts you've just learned in every day practical situations.

If you're in sales, you'll learn how to increase your influence and negotiate more deals.

As a consumer, you'll understand how professional sales-people are using these techniques on you.

TOP TIPS FOR SKILFUL REAL ESTATE NEGOTIATION

■ ■ ■

Making an offer on a property can be an overwhelming experience for many people.

A good real estate agent will be a well-trained and skilful negotiator. In fact, that's one of the core strengths they bring to the table for their clients. The agent can remain objective and calm, while pushing for the best price on the best terms.

On the other hand, most property buyers will be emotional, and this means they will struggle to make rational decisions. They are, after all, negotiating over their 'dream home', their so-called 'castle', and will be spending a lot of money in the hope of securing it. This makes most buyers decidedly emotional and highly vulnerable to paying too much.

This is particularly the case if you haven't engaged a buyer's agent to level the playing field for you. However, help is at hand. Let's start with…

Five questions to ask before you start negotiations

We all want to buy our next home or investment property at the lowest price possible. On the other hand, the vendor wants the highest price he or she can get.

And you now know that the asking price quoted by the selling agent will usually be more than the owner is willing to take for their home. It's part of the real estate game: vendors know the asking price will come down as part of the negotiation process so they list it slightly higher than they would accept and then hope for the best.

So how much should you offer when negotiating your next investment property? Well if you ask the selling agent what price you should offer, you're asking the wrong person.

Remember, the agent is paid by the seller to represent them and to get the best price possible.

Despite that, I would still ask them what they would consider was a 'fair offer' and then ask them to justify it with a list of comparable sales. You don't need to respond to their ballpark figure either. In fact, I would listen without giving much away. At the very least, you should try not to respond with, 'Are you joking?' if you feel the price is too high. You want to remain calm and neutral the whole way through.

If you're thinking that the agent just wants to make a sale, in many cases you are right. In reality the agent doesn't get paid unless a sale is made, so obviously they are keen to sell you the house. Most selling agents prefer an easy negotiation, knowing that sellers can get offended and take it personally when they receive low offers on their homes.

This means they will probably recommend you make an offer close to the asking price. So unless you use a buyer's agent, like my team at Metropole, to help you negotiate, you are really going to have to rely on your own research to work out what the property is worth.

This isn't easy, so take your time to prepare and plan your approach.

In most markets (other than during boom times), houses sell for considerably less than their asking price. There is no standard discount, but as everyone knows there will be some back and forth about the price as agents tend to list the property for sale at an asking price usually about 5–10%more than the market is willing to pay and the seller is willing to accept.

This means the asking price is just a starting point for the negotiations. If you pay what the seller is asking straight off the bat, you are more than likely wasting money.

The trick is to know how much less the seller will accept. So before deciding on what price to offer, here are five questions you should consider asking:

1. How did the vendor come to the asking price for their home?

Was it from the agent's suggestion or because that's how much they need to buy their next dream home? Some sellers are unrealistic and unlikely to come down from their asking price if they have to get a certain amount for a particular reason. It's good to know if this is the case so you don't waste your time and energy.

2. Have there been any other offers made?

This lets you know if you have any competition and how serious the vendor is about selling their home for a reasonable price.

3. How long has the home been on the market?

If it's just been put up for sale, the seller may not be anxious to accept the first offer. On the other hand, if the home has been on the market for several months it's more likely the seller would be ready to accept your offer.

4. Why is the vendor selling?

Are they going through a divorce? Do they have to move interstate urgently? Have they already bought another home that would put them under pressure to sell their current home?

This will let you know how motivated the seller is. I usually save this question towards the end of the conversation with the agent, once a rapport has been established. I find agents tend to open up more about the seller's reason for listing the home, once they have warmed up a little.

5. Has the asking price been reduced during the time the property has been on the market?
This will tell you whether the seller is really keen to offload their home and also let you know that you might have a motivated seller on your hands and perhaps greater bargaining power.

These questions are important because they teach you the art of listening. Remember, negotiation isn't about talking; it's about hearing the response from the other party, both verbal and non-verbal, and using that information to negotiate.

Listening carefully gives you little clues that provide an insight into the other party, and if you have poor listening skills, ultimately you will also have poor negotiation skills.

Now let's look at my top 21 tips to swing the balance more in your favour…

1. KNOW WHAT YOU WANT BEFORE NEGOTIATING

I've already explained the importance of knowing the result you want — your bottom line — before commencing negotiations.

It's a bit like when you're planning your holiday. Firstly, decide your destination — where you want to end up — then work backwards to decide the best way to get there.

In negotiations, as in life, if you don't have a plan of your own, you'll become part of someone else's.

2. KNOW THEIR MOTIVATION FOR SELLING

Vendors sell for a variety of reasons, so it's important to understand what the other side really wants from the negotiation.

And don't be surprised if it's not just about wanting as much money as possible. In fact, many sellers are happy to lower their price if their needs can be met elsewhere. Maybe they want a long settlement or a flexible settlement date?

When you determine what motivates them by asking the agent the right questions then you can give them exactly what they need so you'll be able to get more of what you want.

3. PRICE IS NOT THE ONLY NEGOTIATING FACTOR

We tend to think price is the main negotiating point in property, but there are many other important factors, such as terms and conditions, inclusions and settlement date.

Put yourself in the seller's shoes and once you understand their motivation it will help you put forward a deal that better suits their needs. If the couple is splitting and wants to get out of the house as quickly as possible, a short settlement may be more important than a few extra dollars they would have to split with the spouse they don't like anyway.

On the other hand, if the vendor hasn't purchased their next home yet, a longer settlement may suit them as it would give them the time and flexibility to search for their next home.

4. DON'T LET EMOTIONS GET IN THE WAY

Always leave your ego, as well as your emotions, out of the equation. The better a negotiator you are, the less emotion you will show.

As I've already taught you, the best negotiators realise they must care — but not too much. Not only are they always professional in their dealings, they never take anything personally.

And they understand that even though the vendor is selling the property, it's the agent that they will be dealing with, so it makes no sense to offend them.

You may secretly dislike the agent, they may have a manner or style you dislike, but you cannot let that get in the way of negotiations.

5. NEGOTIATION STARTS THE MOMENT YOU OPEN YOUR MOUTH

Selling agents are highly trained negotiators and they size you up from the moment they meet you. They are assessing you to ensure they don't waste time and effort on someone who is unlikely to make an offer or is merely there to 'sticky beak'. Remember, agents only have one commodity (other than the properties they're selling) and that's their time so they guard it preciously.

If you are genuinely interested, show it. Tell the agent you like the property. Be open, honest and transparent about the extent of your interest, but don't talk money upfront and definitely don't tell the agent the extent of your budget or finance pre-approval.

But I would add a note of caution here: do not gush if you love the home. Express your interest, but never show that you are ruled by your heart rather than your budget. Agents love buyers who do this because they're more likely to go to the top or their budget (or beyond).

On the other hand, don't go too far in the other direction either. It's never a good move to trash a home so the agent thinks you're not interested. Not only is that bad negotiating, it's also just plain rude. And of course, it's unlikely you'll be updated when the agent gets new listings for sale.

6. KNOW MORE THAN THE OTHER PARTY

By now you know that knowledge is power when it comes to negotiation, so before you enter into any property negotiation ensure you know the local market, you've researched which properties have recently sold and for how much, and what hasn't sold and why.

Don't rely on online research as photos are deceptive and homes can look very different in reality than they do using a wide-angle camera lens.

When comparing other properties that have recently sold, focus on elements such as aspect, street appeal, elevation, finishes, quality of construction, position, and whether or not it is close, but not on, a main road. Some of these factors are invisible online, and yet they have a big impact on the value of a property.

And of course, when researching, compare like with like. Focus your attention on a market segment that is similar to the one you are interested in buying. If you are looking to purchase a townhouse then focus solely on this style of home. Ignore houses and apartments as they won't be relevant to your search.

Having this information gives you negotiating power.

7. ENSURE YOU GET THE LAST CONCESSION

Remember, negotiation is a game of asking for and offering concessions.

Whenever you make a concession ensure you always get something in return. The seller wants $700,000, so you offer $650,000. They counter with $675,000 so you agree as long as it's subject to finance.

8. DON'T SPLIT THE DIFFERENCE

One of the most common negotiating techniques agents will use on you is 'let's split the difference'.

Let's say the vendor has dropped their price to $700,000 and your offer was $640,000, they'll suggest you meet halfway at $670,000. It's tempting to accept this — it sounds fair, after all — but don't fall into this trap.

Instead say, 'Thanks, but I just can't. I really can't go over $650,000.' You'll be surprised how often your lower offer gets accepted.

If this doesn't work then another approach is to increase your offer by small increments.

For example, after your initial counteroffer of $650,000 your next offer would be of a lower increment, say $5,000, to $655,000, and your offer after that to $657,250.

Each offer should go up in decreasing amounts as this suggests to the seller that you're running out of steam and they had better accept your offer.

As part of this strategy it's also wise to use the power of time and delay when making the next incremental offer. Don't rush straight back with a counteroffer as this adds to the impression that you're running out of momentum. You really want to give the impression that you're thinking about it (which you are, after all).

9. PROVIDE AN EXPLANATION FOR YOUR OFFER

When you make an offer, it's always a good idea to explain your thinking because this will influence the agent and the seller's expectations about what you're prepared to pay.

It will also usually soften their response when they make a counteroffer.

You could say, for example, that you're offering a lower price than what is listed to account for some renovations that you think are necessary.

For example, your first offer might be based on the lowest recent comparable sale of a property in the area, less an amount of say $20,000. You would then justify this discount based on defects in the property you're buying.

If you get to the stage of making counter offers, attempt to validate these counter offers in the same way. This will give your negotiating more credibility and force.

And if you don't think the property has any defects, you need to look harder. No property is perfect, and you should understand what the negatives are of every property you make an offer on so you can use this information to your advantage.

10. DON'T GO IN TOO LOW

Making an offer which is too 'low ball' can sometimes make the agent think you're just a tyre kicker. It also insults the seller and can prompt them to refuse to deal with you after that.

Therefore, the amount of your first offer is a balance between your desire to secure the property at the best price possible, and presenting an offer that is credible, but without being offensive to the seller so you can start a round of negotiations.

This is where giving a rational basis for the offer, as discussed above, is important.

11. THE HIGHER AUTHORITY TRICK

The tactic of having to consult a 'higher authority' before moving forward with negotiations can work well when buying real estate. Our team of buyers' agents at Metropole use this strategy all the time.

Even though we understand our client's budget and we have our client's authority to proceed, often we will stall the negotiation and say something like: 'Sorry I don't have the authority to proceed higher than $600,000, I'll have to get authority from my client to go higher.'

Lacking the final say in a negotiation can put you in a very powerful position. It puts a temporary pause to the negotiations and allows you some thinking time.

If you're acting for yourself, you can always blame your partner and say that you cannot act any further without clearing it with them as 'you hadn't discussed a higher figure'.

12. NEGOTIATE THE CONDITIONS

Agents operate on the principle that 'less is yes'. That means the fewer conditions that you put in your offer, the greater the chance they have of getting a yes from the seller, and an acceptance of your offer.

But that doesn't mean you should work on the same principle.

From your perspective as a buyer, a simple offer to buy a property on a 10% deposit, settlement in 45 days, cash unconditional will work against you, as the only thing you can negotiate over is the price.

Instead experienced negotiators might make their offer subject to finance, a building and pest inspection, a 120-day settlement and much smaller deposit. This will allow them the opportunity to negotiate away some of these trivial requests that they don't really want, ultimately arriving at a settlement with a 10% deposit, 45-day settlement and fewer bells and whistles, but at a reduced price.

13. PROTECT YOURSELF USING CONDITIONAL CLAUSES

If you're serious about purchasing a particular property, and you don't want to let somebody else outbid you, it's often best to make your offer as simple and clean as possible.

Using the tactic above of adding a heap of conditions to your offer may give you negotiating power, but it could also frustrate the seller who will accept a simpler offer if it's available.

In these cases, a simple but very powerful condition we use is: 'This sale is conditional upon the purchaser's solicitor's approval.'

You'd be surprised how few vendors baulk at this clause yet, if you think about it, your solicitor will not approve the contract proceeding if the building and pest inspection is not to your satisfaction, or if the bank doesn't approve your loan or in fact if you change your mind and tell your solicitor that you don't want them to approve the deal.

It's a simple sounding clause but it covers a lot of ground and really protects you.

14. ALWAYS HAVE AN ALTERNATIVE

A great source of power in property negotiation is telling the agent that you are seriously looking at another property (through another agent who is going to earn the commission).

Don't be too smug about it, if you're interested in a particular property the agent should believe you are keen, but not too keen.

They may ask you for details of the property but be wary of giving too much away. Tell them it's a similar home in a similar neighbourhood and you're 'obviously weighing up the best option'.

15. PATIENCE IS A VIRTUE IN NEGOTIATION

Once you've made an offer it's important to wait for the seller's response. Don't be tempted to make a further offer without hearing from the vendor.

To make another offer is to send a strong message to the seller that you're keen and they will probably take advantage of you, so stay away from your phone until you hear back.

16. TAKE YOUR TIME

In all negotiations, it's important to look as if you have all day, even if you don't. Never say, 'Let's cut to the chase' as this could be perceived as disrespectful to the other party's needs.

Remember, you must play the game so that the other party feels that they've gotten a good deal.

Statements like this send a clear message that you're too willing and overly keen and you could end up at the bottom of the food chain, consumed by the more experienced and sometimes predatory negotiator.

17. NEVER ATTACK THE PROPERTY OR SELLER

Avoid trying to put a negative spin on the property and never get personal during the negotiations. Likewise, if you are genuinely keen, don't act uninterested.

For example, don't describe the property as a 'dog box', a 'demolition job' or a 'haven for drug dealers and prostitutes'. Don't turn your nose up at the area, the quality of the appliances or the furniture.

None of these comments are likely to achieve a reduction in the price and the agent won't take you seriously if they don't think you like the property. Don't forget that sellers want to think their home will be well looked after once they have handed it over to someone else. It's a sentimental thing for them.

You're better off if you advise the seller that the property clearly has potential, but it's obviously in need of work to bring it up to its best condition (which will cost say $40,000) and your offer has been adjusted accordingly.

18. ALWAYS SUBMIT YOUR OFFERS IN WRITING

I might be stating the obvious, but by putting your offer in writing with a small deposit cheque (even a few thousand dollars) formalises the offer and creates a powerful incentive for the agent to hand the seller.

It's easy to throw a number around with an agent, but a written offer shows you are serious.

19. PLACE A TIME LIMIT ON YOUR OFFER

Always place a time limit (say by 5pm Friday afternoon) on your written offer. This can be a powerful negotiating strategy, which lets the vendor know they need to make a decision within that timeframe or risk losing the offer altogether.

20. BE PREPARED TO WALK AWAY

Before entering any negotiation, always know your bottom line and the point at which you will walk away.

The most skilful negotiators are prepared to walk away if the deal doesn't go their way.

At times this is easier said than done, but the best negotiators know that there are plenty more deals out there, so they don't let themselves become emotionally attached. Be nonchalant and let the agent know you have other options.

Remember: it's important that the other side never think that their property is your favourite or that you don't have other options.

21. THE BEST NEGOTIATION TECHNIQUE IS...

I've outlined a few of the many strategies you could use to negotiate a better deal, but at the end of the day, the best negotiation technique is the one where you end up buying the property.

I've seen too many 'smart' investors dig their heels in and lose out on buying a great property for the sake of a few thousand dollars.

Remember you make your money in the long-term not because you buy a property cheaply — that's only a once-off profit — but because you buy the right property, an 'investment-grade' property that keeps delivering wealth and producing high rates of return over many years.

And that is not worth losing this long-term profit because you want to save a few dollars today.

In Australia many of the best properties are sold by auction, so in the next chapter we'll look at how agents use many of the persuasion techniques we've already discussed on you and how you can handle them once you understand them.

HOW TO NEGOTIATE LIKE A PRO WHEN BUYING REAL ESTATE AT AUCTION

■ ■ ■

The property purchase tips in the last chapter related to sales by what is called private treaty. But what if the property you're after is up for sale by auction, as is so common in Australia? You'll need a very different set of negotiating techniques and that's what I'm going to share with you based on the experience my team and I have gained buying hundreds of properties at auction for clients and ourselves.

Of course, real estate agents love selling at auction because they can control the selling environment and use many of the techniques I've already shared with you to maximise the price they achieve for their client — the vendor — and eek the last cent out of the buyer (you).

If you're an agent, this chapter will be useful for you to ensure you understand how to use many of the principles in this book to succeed at auction, or post-auction negotiations. If you're a buyer, it will help to ensure you are aware of the psychological principles used by agents, so you don't become 'shark bait'.

Now I know that many people are a little intimidated by the thought of bidding for a property at auction. I can understand why. Auctions are an emotional and exciting event. Even after bidding at hundreds of auctions I must admit I still get that surge of adrenaline every time I bid.

Then of course there's the lead up to the auction with all the suspicion surrounding what the vendor really wants for his property; is the agent under quoting and enticing you to come along on the day, how much competition will there be?

Or the heartbreak many people feel when falling in love with a property just to be outbid by someone with deeper pockets.

But if you avoid properties that are up for sale at auction, you're going to miss out on a lot of good buying opportunities as usually the best properties are offered for sale by auction, particularly in Melbourne and Sydney. Currently, the team at Metropole buy many properties for our clients at auction.

Fact is, I like auctions. I believe if you've got a good property for sale the auction process is usually the best way to sell it and on the other hand auctions are the most transparent way to buy property.

You see...I like to know who else is interested in the property and what they're prepared to pay. I like that I can see my competition and read their body language. I watch for the signs that they are close to their limit.

Of course, I know many buyers don't see auctions this way. They see them as highly stressful events and they're worried that they may pay more than they intended to in the spur-of-the-moment excitement.

This only happens when you're unprepared. However, if you've done your pre-auction due diligence, such as getting your finance in order, doing a building and pest inspection, checking the contract and prices and determining your maximum price, you can just consider the auction as the venue where you execute the decision you've already made.

And, of course, you must be aware of the little tricks the agent will use on you, so let's first look at some of the psychological principles that we've already discussed and how smart agents and auctioneers use them before, during and after an auction campaign to get through your barriers and work on your subconscious, then I'll share some tactics to help you win at auctions.

Psychological Tricks Agents Use

1. SOCIAL PROOF

Smart selling agents understand that the concept of 'social proof' is a way of easing the minds of worried potential purchasers, so they're keen to show buyers that there are many other people similar to them who are also interested in the property.

After all, *all* of these people gathered at the home can't be wrong, can they?

So prior to the auction they conduct open for inspections at specific times to ensure that there are multiple interested parties going through the property at the same time. They also make sure all the neighbours know the property is for sale to ensure a large crowd gathers on auction day — again adding social proof that this must be a great property.

And of course, when you see other potential buyers bidding against you, you tend to think 'this must be a good property' or 'the price must be fair', otherwise other people wouldn't be bidding, and you feel reassured.

It's an extremely effective technique as we tend to look to other people for validation regarding what we should and should not buy, and this is especially the case with property.

2. SCARCITY

Selling agents know that we value things that are, or at least seem to be, scarce. So let's look at how they use this knowledge to encourage you to make that extra bid or two at auction.

In their preamble you'll often hear the auctioneer explain how rare it is to find a property like this. At times they will 'manufacture' perceived scarcity by playing up the attributes of the property.

Another way to create scarcity is by having the property auction on site, where there's only one property for sale, rather than in an auction room where multiple properties are for sale, one after the other.

If it's a period property, even better., They will wax lyrical about how they don't make homes like this anymore and talk about the 'character' of the home, its period-era details, its uniqueness.

The auctioneer will play on purchasers' emotions by creating scarcity and FOMO (fear of missing out), suggesting the property is just about to be 'knocked down' as he calls for final bids for the first, second and the third call.

Then they'll say something like: 'Don't come to me on Monday and ask if I have another property like this for sale, because I don't.'

They do, of course. No two properties are *exactly* alike, but the real fear they're playing on is that you'll never find another home that you love as much. Which is not true, obviously, but the aim is to make you panic about missing out.

Have you ever noticed the way auctioneers will talk about the successful bidder as having 'won' the auction? Now that's a very clever tactic, because it makes you feel good.

3. RECIPROCITY

I've already explained the principle of giving your customers something before you ask anything of them, but to jog your memory, it relies on the fact we tend to return good deeds.

I've seen agents expertly use this principle by placing coffee trucks outside the house prior to an auction offering attendees free coffee, or agents working with the auctioneer handing out chocolates, lollipops or other treats to members of the crowd or their children.

These actions make you positively predisposed to talking to the agents, working with the agents and bidding at the auction.

4. ANCHORING

This is that cognitive bias tendency where we rely too heavily on an initial piece of information (the 'anchor') when making decisions about the quality or worth of something. Someone drops the anchor by mentioning a figure, and immediately we think the worth of the object is in this ballpark.

First impressions can be hard to shake because we tend to selectively filter, so anchoring bias can influence how much you're willing to pay. The effect works because when you're given a figure, such as the advertised asking price for a property or a suggested end sale price at auction, you are likely to, whether knowingly or not, anchor your judgement by using the number as a reference point (i.e. the anchor).

That's why the auctioneer is likely to say something like 'properties like this one generally sell for $1.5 million'. Now the auctioneer didn't lie, but that doesn't mean that this particular property is worth $1.5 million. However, he has anchored that figure in your mind, and it is likely to impact on how you bid. At least he hopes so!

And don't be surprised if the auctioneer repeats that anchoring price during the auction at a time when the bidding has stalled below that figure of $1.5 million. He's just trying to trick your brain by reminding it of that initial high price it was thinking about.

Today there is legislation in each state of Australia governing how agents quote a potential selling price or how they give a price guide (as the vendor's asking price is not revealed before auction).

Yet I've found that smart agents begin the process of anchoring a potential sale price long before auction day. It starts during the selling campaign when potential purchasers ask the agent what they think the property will sell for.

You'll find the agent saying something like: 'The price we're quoting is $X, but already we've already had strong interest at $Y.'

The way to counteract this anchoring bias is to come to the auction prepared with your own independent research of the property's value and not be biased by what you hear the auctioneer say, or by what other's bid — remember they are unlikely to be as well-informed as you are or as skilled in negotiations.

5. LOSS AVERSION

Loss aversion is another form of cognitive bias where the pain of losing something is psychologically two or three times as powerful as the pleasure of gaining something. In other words, the pain we feel from losing is much more severe than the pleasure we feel from winning an equal amount.

A good auctioneer will understand your fear of losing out the opportunity to purchase a property that you've already considered yours and have possibly spent money on in the form of building inspections.

They play on this fear in a number of different ways during auction.

If the auction, for example, fails to reach the reserve price required for it to sell, a good auctioneer will say, 'If you don't bid now you'll lose the opportunity to negotiate with us to purchase this property', framing the situation as something you are going to lose, rather than saying, 'If you do bid now you will have the opportunity to negotiate with us.'

Other phrases I've heard auctioneers use to tug on our emotions include:

'If you let somebody else buy this property now you'll be out looking at auctions again next weekend.'

'If you don't bid now you'll wake up tomorrow morning regretting that somebody else has bought *your* house.'

'I know your wife is shaking her head saying "Don't bid any higher", but you know that when you get home you'll be in trouble!'

6. RECENCY BIAS

'Recency bias' is the phenomenon of a person most easily remembering something that has happened recently, compared to remembering something that may have occurred a while back.

This means buyers are inclined to make future decisions based on immediate past events, believing future outcomes will directly correlate with recent occurrences.

That's why a good auctioneer will use this principle by telling you how much properties in the area have increased in value over the past year.

They won't mention that period five or six years ago when properties failed to increase much in value, but if there was some positive growth in the past few months in particular, you'll be sure to hear about it!

A few other tactics a good auctioneer will use

Auctioneers will often encourage you to pay more by saying things like, 'Owning a home in this street will be an excellent investment'.

What are they getting at? Well, they're playing on the fact that you're more likely to put your hard earned money into an 'investment' rather than just frivolously paying for an expensive home for your family, even if you are planning to live in the property rather than renting it out as an investment.

Auctioneers will often minimise amounts there are asking you to bid so it seems easier for you to digest. For example, if the current bid is at $750,000, then rather than asking you to bid $755,000 they will ask if you have got another $5,000 in your pocket. Or even another $1,000. They are hoping by not mentioning the full amount they are asking for — the $755,000 — that you'll forget just how much you're paying.

I've also heard a smart auctioneer use the line: 'It's only money. You know it will be worthless in the future.'

Of course, a good auctioneer will be using many or all of these techniques to encourage you to bid more, and the potential combined effect of these statements is staggering.

To avoid falling into these traps auctioneers set for us, we should make ourselves aware of these biases and recognise that we are not the rational decision makers that we think we are.

However, once we know the tricks, understand our own bias, the fears that are played on, we can take a step back and ensure we don't fall prey to the techniques.

Preparing to buy at auction

Of course you can make an offer prior to the auction day, and I'll discuss this in a moment, but let's start with what to do if the property you want to buy goes to auction. And remember, buying at auction is an unconditional sale so here's how you should prepare, because like all other negotiations, if you're well prepared, you'll be more empowered.

Pre-Auction Due Diligence

1. Have your purchasing entity organised (maybe you're buying in the name of a trust, a company or an SMSF, etc.) if you are not buying in your own name.
2. Get a finance preapproval so you know your budget and attend the auction ready to write a deposit cheque.
3. Attend many auctions to experience the atmosphere and observe different bidding strategies.

4. You should ask the selling agent who the auctioneer is going to be (it's rarely the agent you'll be dealing with) and then watch this particular auctioneer in action to learn his individual techniques and the words he uses.

5. Do your research by inspecting many properties and seeing what they sell for (not just the asking price).

6. Know the market, know the value of the property in question and be armed with that power so you can identify a 'walk-away' price — the highest price you're prepared to pay.

7. You should go to the auction with three prices in mind:

    a. The *bargain price* — the figure you'd really love to pay (but know this is unlikely).

    b. The *fair market value* — what you think the property is really worth.

    c. Your *walk away price* — this should be a little higher that the market value if it's a great property. Remember…the best negotiating tactic is the one where you end up buying the property.

8. Play your cards close to your chest. Real estate agents are very skilled at prying information out of potential purchasers, including the price they're prepared to pay for a property. After all — that's their job! Sometimes you can end up revealing things to them that you never intended to and that might be detrimental to your negotiation power. By keeping your cards close to your chest and revealing very little about how much you might pay for a home, you maintain an advantage and ensure the agent cannot use your information to sway

another potential buyer or to help the vendor set his reserve price.

9. Get your solicitor to check the contract and organise any amendments to the contract they suggest.

10. Organise a pest and building inspection. This way you won't get any nasty surprises. However, be realistic and recognise that minor defects will exist in most properties. You do not want to nit-pick and have chipped paint on a door to deter you from buying.

11. Consider getting an experienced buyer's agent like the team at Metropole to bid on your behalf and level the playing field. I know I've already suggested this but having a professional, experienced negotiator represent you makes a huge difference.

What to do on the day

1. Arrive early, survey the landscape and see who else is there. Do they look like serious bidders or are they just onlookers? In some states bidders must register so get there early, see who registers their interest and check out your competition. In other states see who's inspecting the contract of sale that's on display and look for those saying the right things.

2. Just to make things clear, your competition is not the auctioneer, even though they will be using all sorts of psychological tricks to encourage you to bid one more time. Your real competition is the other bidders. In fact, it's only the under bidder, the one you must beat by one

more bid to snare that property. Just like the auctioneer is using psychological tricks on you, you should try and 'psyche out' the other bidders and convince them that you've got deeper pockets than they have and that you'll bid higher that they will. Dress like you have the means to buy the property and watch your body language. Stand proud, be assertive and don't look nervous.

3. Stand in a position where you can see everybody, and everybody can see you. Don't hide. Be out near the front where you can watch the body language of the other bidders. Are they nervous, are they conferring with their wife, are they ringing someone on the phone, are they running out of steam?

4. In a strong auction climate use the psychological advantage of projecting confidence — make the other bidders think you have deep pockets and no limit.

5. Don't be afraid to look other bidders straight in the eye and make sure you bid confidently in a loud, clear voice.

6. You should always be the first bidder and show you're serious by making a firm and high bid near what you think the reserve price is. The property won't sell below this and make your bids fast and assertive. I know many people start their bidding low but when you think are about it, the property won't be sold below its reserve, so all that happens when you bid low is you give the auction some momentum with multiple bids. I'd rather knock out the other tentative purchasers right from the start with a strong bid.

7. Procrastinating or agonising over your next bid is a sign of weakness. Call out your offer in full. In other words, say $750,000 instead of the increments — don't just say $5,000. Make your last bid as loud and assertive as the first.

8. Be prepared to miss out. Stick to your 'walk-away' price.

9. If the property is going to pass in, make sure you are the highest bidder, as this allows first right to negotiate with the vendor.

10. If you miss a property at auction, accept that it wasn't meant to be and look forward to finding something better soon.

11. While no one likes to consider themselves the 'loser' in any sort of negotiation campaign, it's far better to walk away and live to fight another day than over-commit to a property you've become emotionally blinded by.

12. Don't forget, if you're too nervous you can also authorise someone else to bid on your behalf. Obviously, I'm biased but having a buyers' agent like my team at Metropole represent you levels the playing field and gives you an edge.

Six auction sins

Clearly auctions can be a psychological battle, so it's important to have a strategy in place to give you the best chance of winning on the day. But this is no different to any other major negotiation is it? This means there are some things you shouldn't do at auctions — blunders that could cost you that psychological edge.

1. Not bidding at all

It's interesting that many prospective buyers just don't want to make a bid, and some even let the property pass in to another buyer. Then they'll hang around after the auction, hoping a deal isn't reached so they can jump in and negotiate the bargain of the century — alas, this is usually a terrible tactic.

The only way to be the winner at the end is to actually bid. As I said, be the first bidder and make sure you're the last one to bid because then either you end up buying the property or if it passes in, you can negotiate with the seller.

2. Deciding on a round number

Never finish your bidding on a round number, because most bidders set their limit on a round number. This means one or two more small increments could win you the property. So rather than setting in upper limit of $750,000, set yours at $753,000— two bids above where others may stop.

Many bidders set an inflexible limit, and often a round number such as $700,000, for no valid reason. I've seen buyers miss out on a property because they're not prepared to increase their bid by as little as $500, which is silly when you think about the long-term capital growth potential they may be missing out on.

As I said, you need to set three prices. The price you'd love to pay. The price you'd be happy to pay. And the price which will really hurt, but once you've snared that property you'll

look back in a few years and it won't hurt — you'll be so
happy you extended yourself to buy that property.

3. Stopping and starting

Buyers who pause mid-auction to confer with their family or
friends about their limit or intentions could be giving away
more than they know. It's important for a buyer who's there
with their partner to decide on who's actually bidding and
also to determine key signs to allow you to communicate in
a non-verbal fashion mid-auction.

To become more comfortable, attend as many auctions as you
can to watch the theatre of how successful bidders behave,
their body language and their interaction with the auctioneer.

If you're keen to buy, you need to be assertive even if they're
on your last bid by making it seem like you still have several
bids up your sleeve.

4. Asking if the property is 'on the market'

Auctions are a form of street theatre and you'll find the initial
bids are usually well below the seller's 'reserve price' and
the property will not sell until this figure (or an amended
reserve price) is reached. That's when the auctioneer will
advise the property is 'on the market' or 'we're now going to
sell the property'.

Sometimes nervous buyers ask the auctioneer, 'Is it on the
market?' You'll know when the property is on the market.

The auctioneer often will have gone inside to his vendors to confer if they are prepared to sell and he'll let you know.

However, it shouldn't matter to you if the property is officially on the market or not, whether it has reached its reserve price or not, because if the seller has gone to the trouble of putting their property to auction they are keen to sell. They have invested time, money and emotion in marketing their property, so in essence it has been 'on the market' for about a month. All you are now doing is negotiating the price. Don't show your hesitancy by asking this question, instead bid to your pre-set limit and hopefully you'll be the winner on the day.

5. Making ridiculous offers
Starting too low with your bidding might, in some cases, invite other bidders into the auction ring and allow momentum to build.

On the other hand, starting with a strong, confident bid could knock out several contenders early on.

If you've done your market research, and hopefully you have, then making a ridiculously low offer is usually a mistake.

6. Pretending you're not interested
It's a strange phenomenon that some buyers attend auctions and then pretend they're not interested in it at all. In my mind it can work in the buyer's favour to show interest during the entire auction campaign.

If no one bids at auction, because seemingly they're not interested, then the vendor is legally entitled to make a vendor bid on the property to help move the auction along.

This can either get things started or be used when the auction stalls because everyone is trying to 'play the game'.

Agents say however that they want to help a genuine buyer purchase the property, so it's important to be upfront about your intent in the pre-auction days. It's always better to be a standout potential buyer because it can help you compete better on auction day as well as be on the agent's radar.

What to do if you're the highest bidder for a property that is passed in at auction

At an auction, if the property doesn't meet the reserve price, it 'passes in'.

Imagine you turn up to an auction, keen to buy your next home or investment property, the auction stalls and the property is passed in. What do you do?

When a property passes in, the highest bidder is generally given first right to negotiate with the vendor's agent.

The first thing to do is to put yourself in the position to able to negotiate with the vendor and this means you should be the highest bidder. It's not always easy to manipulate the order of the bidding, but it's important to put yourself in that position.

What happens next is the selling agent or auctioneer usually invites you to step inside the property and commence negotiations, while other agents approach the under-bidders to explore their level of interest and keep them 'hot' in case the negotiations with you fall through.

Remember, the agent is acting on behalf of the vendor and it's their job to get the best price for their client and many of them do it very, very well. You can bet your deposit they are highly skilled at emotion-based selling and will employ tactics to make you believe they are going to help you. But no matter how convincing the agent appears, remember they're not on your side.

Now it's time for your negotiating skills to come to the fore.

Unless it is pouring rain do not follow the agent inside. This puts you on their turf and isolates you from what's going on outside. I prefer to stand outside where I can assess whether there is any real competition or just friends who are pretending to be buyers hanging around.

The perceived pressure of having competition outside, breathing down your neck and waiting for an opportunity to negotiate is a powerful negotiation tool that agents use against you.

I've found the tactic of displaying strong body language, standing on my own turf (even though I still might have butterflies in my stomach) surprises the agents and returns the negotiating power to me.

Now the game begins…The first question I ask is, 'What is the vendor's reserve price?'

Remember, the reserve is the minimum price the vendor told the agent (prior to the auction) he or she would accept for their property. But now that the auction has failed they may, in fact, accept a lower price.

So when you hear the reserve price you should baulk (remember the *flinch*), seem surprised at how high it is and ask: 'I understand that's the price the vendor was hoping for before the auction, but NOW what is the lowest price they will sell for?'

You next steps will depend on what the vendor wants for their property and what you believe it is worth based on your pre-auction research.

If you're like me, you'll have an estimate of what the property is worth under low competition (what you'd really like to buy it for) and then the maximum you would be prepared to pay under intense competition (such as if the auction had continued on).

Of course, just because the property has been passed in doesn't mean that this is the market price, it is simply a starting point for further negotiation.

The real market value is what you and hopefully the vendor have assessed it to be based on comparable sales evidence.

The key is to work within the price range you, and only you, have determined and not waver from it. What happens next really depends at which end of your price range the property is passed in for. If it is at the lower end you have more flexibility and knowing if there is any competition waiting outside will influence how flexible you are.

I would say something like, 'I've already offered you the upper end of what I think the property is worth', even if it's not the case.

Obviously, if there are no other buyers waiting in the wings you can minimise the amount you are willing to counter-offer.

Now don't fall into the trap of making the same counter increments as the vendor. Often the agent will ask you to meet the vendor halfway, but obviously you're not obliged to do so.

Stick to your guns and your own method of negotiation — that one that aligns with your interests — and don't let someone else's negotiation techniques or tactics throw you off and cause you to make a decision you'll later regret.

6 times you can snag a property before auction

Sometimes a smart negotiating technique is to try and buy a property before it goes to auction. This works particularly well when our property markets are a little slow, when auction clearance rates are dropping, and when vendors are getting nervous.

This means that it's possible to buy good properties before they even make it to auction day. There are several reasons why vendors may be open to selling before auction day. Some of the most common ones are:

1. Nervous vendors

There's nothing quite like the energy at an auction. It's a tense, exciting atmosphere. But some vendors just can't handle it.

So to avoid auction day nerves entirely, some sellers opt to sell before the big day.

This is great news for you if you're looking to buy, because you can play into those nerves (nicely of course) and send them an offer early on.

They might be relieved to avoid the stress of the auction process altogether — and you might have your hands on the house you wanted even sooner!

2. Sensitive sellers

Selling can be a stressful time for the vendor, and if they're particularly sensitive — perhaps they're elderly, or going through an emotional time — the thought of going to auction might create too much of an emotional rollercoaster for them.

Depending on their circumstances, they might need to sell fast and move swiftly, so receiving an offer before auction could actually save them a lot of time and stress.

Remember…you're not taking advantage of the people; you're taking advantage of the situation. You'll be assisting the vendor by relieving their stress.

3. Time is running out

If the seller has already bought a house elsewhere, they could be in a bit of a panic at the thought of being unable to sell their first property in time. No one wants to be paying mortgages for two properties!

By giving them an offer to consider before auction day, you're giving them the opportunity to eliminate the very real risk of the property being passed in at auction — while allowing them to move on with confidence to their new home.

4. There just isn't much interest

No matter how hard real estate agents works to generate interest in a property, sometimes the buyers just aren't biting.

So, if there isn't much excitement or enthusiasm prior to auction, the agent may advise their client to consider any offers that come their way beforehand…which is where you can swoop in to save the day.

Of course, you should take advantage of this situation — a nervous vendor and no or little competition puts you in the driver's seat. You'll be in a great negotiating position.

5. The agent is in a hurry to sell the property

You might find that the agent is very impatient to sell. This can happen if the property has been on the market and has been the agent's listing for a while, or if they're dealing with a particularly tricky seller (yes, it happens!).

Whatever the reason, a hurried agent could be a boon for you, as it means you have the upper hand when it comes to negotiating the best possible deal.

6. You have a premium offer on the table

While we sometimes wish it wasn't the case, let's be honest: money talks.

If you can slide through with a premium offer that no one in their right mind would say no to, then it could secure you the property in a hot second.

One thing to be wary of, is your money talking too much, and raising the bar so high that both the seller and their agent think other similar offers might be made at auction?

This is a risk of putting your best foot forward prior to auction — but it just might pay off.

The only way you'll ever know whether you can snag a property before it goes to auction is by putting the offer out there. The worst the vendor can do is say no, and if that's the case, you can still roll along to the auction when it occurs and try your luck once more.

5 Benefits using a Buyer's Agent

Buying real estate is a big deal. Regardless of how well you think you know the market or how extensively you've researched, every property you settle is a massive milestone.

That doesn't mean every deal should be celebrated, however. We all make mistakes from time to time, and when it comes to buying a home or investment property, your mistakes can be extremely costly in the long run.

Sure, you're learning how to negotiate in this book, but there's another safety net for you — the buyer's agent.

A buyer's agent is a licensed real estate professional who knows the ins and outs of the market. They act on behalf of the buyer to negotiate hard, research extensively, and generally make sure the best choices are made.

Their benefits can be a little murky to quantify, so let's dig deeper and explore what precisely a buyer's agent can do for you.

1. They save you time

In the interest of saving valuable time, a buyer's agent can be an essential part of your property journey. In a nutshell, they spend time researching and then searching for the type of property you've got your heart set on so that you don't have to. No more researching online on your Saturday mornings, hoping you'll come across a diamond in the rough, because now you have a gem that can do it for you.

Once you outline the features you want — from suburb, to aspect and view, to number of bedrooms — your buyer's agent will search on your behalf using your criteria. The countless hours you'll save by hiring a buyer's agent can minimise your stress levels and maximise your chance of successfully finding the property you want — especially if you're buying from interstate or overseas.

2. They have access to a wider range of properties

You know that old saying, 'It's not what you know, it's who you know?'

Well, that applies to the property industry in a big way.

Enlisting the service of a buyer's agent can open you up to a wider range of properties, some of which may not be advertised on the market — now or ever. This puts you in a favourable position as you have access to deals unavailable to the wider public. If you're looking to buy an investment property, this can be especially profitable in a hot market, as your buyer's agent can pounce on deals before motivated buyers peddle prices up.

In fact, well over 35% of the properties the team at Metropole have bought over the last year have been off market or pre-market properties.

3. They're able to negotiate strong deals

Be honest: while you're pretty good at haggling a discount on white goods at Harvey Norman, property is a whole new ballgame — and you're likely to be a rookie.

When you've finally found your perfect property you might think the negotiations will be a breeze, but the experience can be far more intimidating than you anticipated.

A buyer's agent acts without emotion on your behalf, and so will be able to negotiate better terms on that deal for you. They have much more local knowledge on what makes a fair price in comparison to the current market.

Plus, they'll ensure you don't risk spending too much on your prized property purchase.

4. They help you choose the best property

The additional advice and expertise provided by a buyer's agent can also help you make sure you're not getting yourself into a lemon of a property.

While a home might seem perfect on the outside, a buyer's agent knows what to look out for in terms of hidden issues that you might not have otherwise recognised. Your buyer's agent will also ensure the property you end up with is well-aligned with your specific wealth creation goals and investment strategies.

Searching for a renovator so you can add value, but get seduced by the bells and whistles of a new build? Your buyer's agent can keep you on track and remind you of your goals. That way you won't be enticed by deals that may be good value, but they don't quite match your needs.

5. *They help you avoid common mistakes*
Purchasing property can be a risky venture and there are plenty of mistakes that can be made.

A buyer's agent will help by steering you away from making the most common mistakes throughout the whole process — from researching property to signing the contract — as they're able to identify any potential red flags before it's too late.

This is especially helpful if you're planning to bid at auction, which can be an intimidating process.

Having someone with the skills and know-how to successfully bid for you can put you steps ahead of your competitors and take a lot of the pressure off.

While you might be inclined to avoid spending more money than you have to during your road to owning property, enlisting the help of a buyer's agent is a hugely worthwhile payoff.

The results you can achieve from working with qualified professionals far outweigh the costs, as they can save you time, money and stress — and start you on the best path towards property success. And interestingly this is one of the few occasions when you can hire a professional negotiator to work on your behalf to level the playing field.

If you're keen to know more, why not check out the services that my team at Metropole provide — www.Metropole.com.au.

By the way…we're much more than just buyer's agents, we provide strategic wealth and property advice, financial planning, property management, and property renovations and development project management.

In the following chapters I'm going to look at some of the other types of negotiations you'll find yourself in and give you some helpful tips.

SAY WHAT? HOW TO NEGOTIATE WITH LIARS, DIFFICULT PEOPLE AND TYPE A PERSONALITIES

■ ■ ■

There is no doubt that some people are easier to negotiate with than others. This can come down to a personal connection — sometimes we just seem to click well with the person we are negotiating with (we have rapport), while at other times we just don't seem to gel.

No matter how skilled a negotiator you become, you'll doubtless come across people who are tricky to do a deal with. These people require delicate handling and you need to be extra careful when negotiating with these wily types. I talked about different personality types in the first section of this book and now I am going to talk about handling a breed all of their own: those who are, by their very nature, tough to handle.

I classify these negotiation types into three broad groups: Liars, Type A Personalities and Difficult People.

LIAR, LIAR

Firstly, I want to touch briefly on the topic of dealing with liars.

We're all prone to a bit of exaggeration at times. I read one study that found people tell, on average, one or two lies every day. Heck, most real estate agents know the value of adding some mayonnaise, which is why they refer to tiny apartments as 'cozy' and properties on main roads as 'close to transport'.

Negotiators are no exception. Various studies suggest roughly half of those making deals will lie when they have a motive and the opportunity to do so. Typically they see it as a way to gain the upper hand.

It's not always easy to pick lies, especially when they're cloaked in flattery: your boss's promise that a promotion is coming any day now; the supplier's assurance that your order is his top priority. We're wired to readily accept information that conforms to our pre-existing assumptions or hopes.

So let's look at some ways to ensure you're not duped in a negotiation:

How do you know they're lying?
As I said, most of us aren't too good at picking liars, but once you know what to look for, you'll watch for particular speech patterns or body language.

- *Watch their body language* — by now you realise that body language makes up a large part of how we communicate (much more so than words) so pay close attention to the tone and body language of the other party looking for hidden signs such as incongruities.

  A liar may try to put up some sort of barrier between you as a defensive posture. They may cross their arms and legs, point their feet toward the nearest exit, or place something between you and them like a table or chair.

  A liar may unconsciously nod yes while saying no (or vice versa) but be careful…both truthful people and liars can commit these nervous acts, while a practiced liar may not signal deception in a way you can notice.

- *Watch their eyes.* Liars can more easily control their words than their unconscious non-verbal leaks. Often they'll stare at the floor because they can't look you in the eyes, unless they're a really good liar and then they'll make a determined effort to look you in the eyes too much. Another subtle clue is a liar's blink rate increases.

- My ears prick up when someone says '*In all honesty…*' or '*To tell you the truth…*' It usually means they are not being honest or telling the truth.

- Liars often try to *change the subject* or deflect a direct question. They'll mumble or change the topic, saying something like 'I really love my job here', 'Wow, is that a new outfit you're wearing?' They often get around direct questions by answering not what they were asked but what they wish they'd been asked. Unfortunately, listeners usually don't notice these dodges, often because they've forgotten what they originally asked.

- *Can't keep quiet.* I've mentioned the power of silence and taking a pause in negotiation. In fact, there's an adage that states the first one to talk, loses. In the case of lying it seems even more relevant. Most liars hate silences and rush to fill the void with rambling. So keep quiet, remain silent and see if some inane babbling ensues.

Then the way forward is to focus on what you can control. While you can't control whether the other person is lying, or anything else about their behaviour during the negotiation. You can control your own behaviour and decisions.

Don't join the team

When someone displays an outright hostility towards truth and makes things up on the spot, it can be tempting to join them.

After all, they've shown no regard for doing a deal in a professional manner so why should you? All bets are off, right?

Well, no. Never shoot yourself in the foot by lowering yourself to another person's level.

Lying is unethical and it's counterproductive. Tell enough lies in business and you'll get a reputation for being untrustworthy and no one will want to work with you.

Furthermore, lying isn't necessary. If you follow the principles in this book, and work on the skills outlined, then you'll become an expert negotiator, who is well respected for telling the truth and behaving ethically. You can have both, you see.

Call them out

Negotiating expert Chris Voss teaches that there are three kinds of yes that you will hear during negotiations: commitment, confirmation, and (most commonly) counterfeit.

How should you respond when a yes, or any other answer, sounds hesitant? Call it out and respond by using one of these statements:
'You sound a little hesitant...'
'That yes sounds a little hesitant...'
'It sounds like there is something else on your mind...'

Another way to call it out is to ask for proof.

For example, an agent may go on and on about how much interest there is in a property and if you don't put an offer in now you'll miss out to the three or four other buyers who are currently fighting over it.

In this instance, ask for specifics. When people are lying, they become extremely vague, their story will jump ahead in time and there will often be very little detail.

Ask the real estate agent to provide details of the offer. How much and when? If the agent is in fact lying, it will become clear, very quickly.

Get as much as you can in writing

Liars love to chat in person, probably because in negotiations it allows them to make all sorts of wild claims that can then go unchecked and unrecorded.

They can later deny a figure they gave to you or backtrack on a claim that was agreed upon in person.

That's why it helps to nail down specifics in writing or by email. If there is an area of contention that you fear the other party may be cagey on then get it in writing.

Most real estate transactions involve a contract, but in other negotiations, whether it be with a boss or with a utilities company, a written outline is a great way to hold people to account and flush out any liars.

Re-state the terms

As I mentioned above, liars trade on vagueness and hate specifics. This is where you need to be as clear as possible about the nuts and bolts of a negotiation.

When dealing with people who don't always tell the truth, make sure you outline what is at stake (what is being negotiated), what your offer is, any conditions, and a timeline for proceeding.

This not only gives you peace of mind but it sends a very clear message to the liar that you are not to be trifled with and will not just let things slip by.

Avoid where possible

Finally, if you can, avoid dealing with liars. It's really that simple. The best way to do business with unethical types is to avoid them all together.

Luckily, in business most people realise that their reputation is all they've got. Their word matters and so they make sure they stick to it.

Where you can avoid dealing with liars, do so. Otherwise, don't let their lack of respect for truth rattle you.

Be suspicious of what they say, ask lots of questions, and get it all in writing. By assuming everything they say is false, you'll be spared any nasty surprises.

Now let's look at other ways you may have to deal with difficult people.

TYPE A PERSONALITIES

Let me start by saying that Type A personalities are not the same as liars. Just because I am placing them in the hard to handle basket doesn't place them in the same category as liars.

A Type A person has a temperament characterised by excessive ambition, aggression, competitiveness, drive, impatience, need for control, focus on quantity over quality and an unrealistic sense of urgency. They often view the world with a 'dog eat dog' mentality.

This means Type As are hard to handle because they're usually extremely good at everything they do. They're competitive and love to win. In fact, winning is extremely important to them, which can be a big problem if *you* are the one trying to win.

They're often in a hurry, stressed and extremely assertive. The best way to describe Type A is that they are the exact opposite of chilled — no one would ever call them relaxed.

I am Type A myself, so I used to have a hard time dealing with Type As. I put up a good fight, until I learned to turn their biggest strengths into weaknesses and gently pull them where I want them to go.

So how do you negotiate with them? You let them 'win'. OK, let me clarify that a little by saying that you will only let them think they've won. The beauty of 'winning' is that it's relative and has no set standards.

For example, if you're negotiating the purchase of an expensive item from a Type A vendor, you need to let them think they've got a great price for their product or service. Anchor your initial offer quite low and then begrudgingly come up over a series of negotiations that makes the other party think you've gone higher than you want to. Your final offer should be a very specific one: $876,450, for example. This tells the Type A vendor that you have reached your limit. That will make them, and their competitive spirit, extremely happy.

I have found that in many negotiations there is one party that gets the financial payoff and the after party who gets the psychological payoff. One important way you can let Type A personalities feel they've won is to give them the psychological 'feel good' of being smarter, brighter, more articulate and more worldly than you are.

Congratulate them on their great negotiation skills. What they don't need to know is that you were, in fact, quite a way off your limit. As you're a skilled negotiator, you're able to let them feel that they've won, while secretly knowing you're the real winner.

Winning is relative to the situation at hand. You simply have to create a situation where them winning means you get everything you want.

Reflect their behaviour
The world is a frustrating place for many Type As. They're organised, many people aren't. They take things seriously, many people don't. It's quite likely you're a Type A yourself — after all, you're reading this book— and you probably know exactly what I'm talking about.

In order to win their respect and trust, you need to be on your A game with them. Respond promptly to their emails and phone calls (you should be doing this anyway). Outline timelines for completing certain jobs. For example, if you're making a counteroffer, let them know when you'll get back to them.

Be as organised and as switched on as they are, and you'll easily win their trust, which will lead to a better outcome for you. Type As quickly get frustrated with slow and incompetent people.

Do your research

Type As are heavily focused on research and they have always done their homework. That is why you can never take your foot off the pedal with these types.

You need to know the value of your offer, what they're likely to counter-offer, their motivations for selling, and have a plan in place for the negotiation. If you are buying a property off a Type A selle, then it helps to display your knowledge of the market when dealing with them. This will earn their respect and put you in a good position to secure the best deal possible.

Use the power of time

As most Type As feel that there is not enough time in the day and are always rushing from one thing to the next, you can use this fear to your advantage.

As a skilled negotiator, you will be calm and give the impression you have all the time in the world. This is likely to work in your favour as Type As will most likely be in a hurry to get a deal done.

When buying an investment property, you can use this to your advantage by emphasising any other properties you are looking at and your desire to make the right decision. Many Type As will panic at the thought of losing you and may accept a lower offer to secure your business.

You can also show your seriousness by putting a deadline on all your offers: as time rules the lives of many Type As, this is something they will respond to.

DIFFICULT PEOPLE

Now we come to dealing with the most challenging of all the challenging negotiation types: the difficult person. We've all come across this type along our way. They are the person who, through no fault of yours, have decided to make things difficult.

Now, most things don't have to be difficult at all. But some people seem determined to throw obstacles in your path no matter how courteous and respectful you are. Perhaps they're having a bad week, or maybe you remind them of their ex husband or wife.

Honestly, you could waste hours psychoanalysing difficult people and still be none the wiser as to why they behave the way they do. The real point is: how do you manage them?

Keep your cool

Let's begin with what you should never do: don't join them in their misery. That means refraining from yelling, getting hostile or being rude. This will simply make matters worse.

Let's say, for example, you are wanting to negotiate a lower interest rate on one of your properties and the bank has made a number of errors with your account in the past. You hope to use these mistakes as leverage in asking for a lower rate now, but are finding the person on the other end of the phone is rude and dismissive of your request.

Instead of being upset about their tone, you could say, 'I am disappointed in what has happened and in light of the error I think a discount on my rate is wholly justified to retain my business. I would like to stay with your bank and feel that this discount would adequately compensate me and persuade me to stay.'

If the tone doesn't change, then speak to someone else. Be firm about your desire to have it handled by a senior manager.

Invite them to your corner

Sometimes all it takes when negotiating with a difficult person is to get them on side. You can use language that transforms your problem into their problem, so that, all of a sudden, you're going through something together.

If, for example, an airline mess-up has cost you a seat and you're seeking to be moved to an earlier flight, you can use smart language to get your preferred seat or an upgrade.

Use open-ended phrases such as, *'What should we do?'* and *'What options are available for you to use?'* which invites the difficult person to stop seeing problems and find a solution. It changes their perspective and is remarkably effective. Instead of berating them to fix something, you're casually inviting them to use their powers to help you.

Stay put and be silent

This is one of my favourite techniques and I've seen it used to devastating effect over the years. When a difficult person tells you something you're after is not possible then...wait for it... do nothing.

This is most effective when dealing with someone in person. By simply not leaving and remaining quiet, you will become a bigger problem to the person than if you had of stormed off.

Let's take for example, the very simple example of wanting to secure a medical appointment. You ask for the appointment to be on a certain day, but the unfriendly receptionist wants it on a later day as the doctor is already pretty busy on the day. Hold your ground and see what happens. Re-state nicely that you need it on that day and then stand there calmly and wait. You'll be surprised how many times an appointment can be found.

If all else fails...

Sometimes the difficult person is so intent on being miserable that you almost need to shake them out of it.

What I suggest doing in these circumstances is to gently — gently is the word here — acknowledge their behaviour. Sometimes people are so used to treating others however they wish that they need a mirror held up to them.

You could say, *'You seem really stressed, is everything OK?'* Often that is enough to prompt the person to reflect on their behaviour and nine times out of ten they will modify it.

You can try this technique after all else fails but be aware that it can backfire. Some people are intent on creating problems and there is not much you can do about it.

The bottom line:

If you're in sales or management, unfortunately dealing with difficult people is par for the course. You'll be negotiating with or trying to persuade or influence people you mistrust, dislike, or even think are 'evil'. Nonetheless, a skilled negotiator knows where to find and create value in any negotiation.

SHOW ME THE MONEY: HOW TO NEGOTIATE THE SALARY YOU DESERVE

■ ■ ■

If you pay any attention to media stories on the state of the economy, you would be aware that wages are pretty flat in Australia. In fact, most of the developed world is pretty stagnant, with very little growth in the middle class pay brackets in recent times.

In the good old days getting a job was as simple as putting your hand up for one. Many people could take their choice of office jobs, and the public service offered generous leave and superannuation schemes.

Not so anymore. Job security is virtually non-existent and that has led many people to become afraid — too afraid, if you ask me — to ask for a raise.

But this is the wrong way of looking at it. While job security may be gone, that can actually be a good thing for workers who are skilled and know their value. After all, employers have as much to lose when a good worker walks out the door and today's hyper-mobile job market makes that easy to do for those who are in demand.

So it's important to know your worth and this means ensuring you're properly paid for the work you do. There is nothing wrong with taking an interim pay cut at a new job while you establish your credentials and get your foot in the door. But I do think there is something wrong with staying at that pay bracket and not securing a wage rise, once you have proven your value to the company.

Of course, securing a pay rise is not as simple as walking into the boss's office and holding your hand out. You'll need a toolbox of techniques that you can draw on to give yourself the best chance of getting that raise.

Be humble

Before you walk into that office and state your case, ask yourself why you think you deserve one.

Because you need it? Not good enough. Your expenses, like the rest of your personal life, are your business and no one else's — least of all, your boss's.

Unless you believe you have earned that raise, then there is no point in walking in. You will just put your boss offside.

Don't say things like:

- 'I need more money.'
- 'I can't afford my expenses.'
- 'Here's what I made at my last job.'

Instead say:

- 'I'm able to solve X (a problem or a task) and people who can do that are worth $Y in the market.'
- 'The salary range for my position in the market is $X- $Y.'

Start early

Most employees put their boss on the spot when they ask for a raise. Often it's the first that the boss has even heard of the request, and, when under pressure, most people don't react very well. I would start canvassing for a raise, in a subtle fashion, a few months beforehand. Perhaps during your performance review you could highlight how you have gone above and beyond and follow up your examples with general questions as to how raises are decided. That way, your boss won't be surprised when you make a formal request.

Research competitors

I am not a big fan of setting your salary according to industry benchmarks — it often limits what talented staff can ask for — but I think it's important that you know what a person in a similar position as you is getting paid in another company. This allows you to know whether an offer is low or high, according to benchmarked standards.

Show your value

Of course, it's extremely important that you come to the conversation with plenty of examples of your value to the company but be careful not to sound too focused on your own interests. You're part of a team, remember, so emphasise your collegial approach to work and the way you enhance company culture — in addition to what you did for the company's bottom line (because that matters too).

Don't be the first to make a suggestion of your salary increase

Now I know I've previously suggested that smart negotiators make the first offer as this has an 'anchoring' effect. However, I've found staff coming in and saying to me *'I'm looking for $X'* is a terrible strategy that puts me offside. So firstly, show your value as I've just explained and let your employer make the first offer. If you're as valuable as you think you are you may be surprised at what they come up with.

Don't moan about your co-workers

Nothing kills a deal quite like underhand gossiping, and while it may be tempting to dob in the guy in your department who sits on Facebook all day, while citing how hard you work in comparison, never do this. While what you're saying may be true, it's never a good look to bring down a lazy co-worker to bolster your own case. Your boss is unlikely to think higher of you for doing it, and, besides, your work should speak for itself.

Feel free to praise co-workers

Having said that, it's always a good idea to highlight any strong relationships you have in the office with other high-performing colleagues. This not only allows your maturity to shine, it also presses home to your boss how well you work with others and how strong your communication skills and connection to the company are.

Time your request

Make sure you choose your moment when asking for a pay rise, and this means right down to the day and hour that you ask your boss.

Research has shown that as the day progresses, managers experience 'decision-fatigue' whereby they are less likely to say 'no' to proposals later in the day once they are weary from making so many judgment calls. Use this to your advantage by waiting until after lunch, if possible, to chat to your boss. He or she is likely to be less distracted by the early morning rush to respond to emails, but not so tired as to be switched off from work.

Consider the company's position

I would also suggest timing your request for a period when the company has a healthy bottom line. If your request for a pay rise coincides with a poor quarterly performance, it may be worth waiting until the balance sheet improves. However, don't be too obvious about it. If, for example, the company has just announced record profits and you walk in the next day asking for a raise, it may be viewed in a negative light.

Throw in some extra responsibility

If your responsibilities have increased in recent months, then that is an excellent time to raise the issue of pay. You could highlight the extra work you are doing, without making it sound like a burden, and then clearly state that you are happy to do the extra work, but wonder if the additional job responsibilities place the role in a higher pay bracket? If you have not taken on any additional responsibilities then doing so could be a good way of justifying the raise, especially if the extra money you are asking for is a significant amount.

Give your boss time to decide – but not too much time

Depending on the temperament of your boss, you may not be able to get a response from them on the spot. That's OK. If your boss is having trouble making that decision in front of you, then it's time to cut them some slack. Let them know that you don't require a response right away but will check in with them in a few days' time. Always make sure you're clear as to when you'll follow up as you don't want the issue to simply be forgotten.

Prepare for 'no'

While some bosses will agree to give you a raise, others will either say 'no' or put you off without giving you a firm response either way. If this occurs, don't despair. Pay raise negotiations are a work in progress and if your boss gives you a flat-out 'no' try to keep the door open by asking what you would have to do for he or she to change their mind.

Whatever happens, don't get emotional. A 'no' the first time around is not the end of the world, but if you react angrily or defensively then that will ruin your future chances of securing a 'yes'.

As with anything in negotiation: play the long game.

SELLING IN A POST-COVID ENVIRONMENT

■ ■ ■

It's safe to say that thanks to COVID-19 the last few years were like no other I've experienced in my business career and while in many ways life is back to normal, some things will certainly not revert back to the "old normal".

The fright of the pandemic and now the economic challenges the world is experiencing have challenged many of the old ways of selling and have given us a new set of rules moving forward.

For one, there are no more "blind dates".

Your prospects will already know all about you before they come to see you. They have done their research online, they've looked at all the reviews, they've checked out what the competition has to offer and now it's a bit like online dating – they've swiped through all the alternatives before they chose to speak with you.

In the old days it was the salesperson's role to explain all the features and benefits and how their product or service would help the prospect – but it's no longer the salesperson's role to educate – their prospect has already done all their homework.

So what's the role of the salesperson in this new environment?

It's their job to create value.

One of my coaches, Simon Bowen – www.modelsmethod. com.au (I really recommend you check out his models which will transform the way you sell and convert forever) – says there is only one real reason someone buys from you…

It's that you create value for them that they can't create for themselves, or that they don't believe anyone else can create for them in the same way you do. And the value you create must be of much greater value to them than any other value they can create, or get, with the money they spend with you.

So in order to "persuade" someone to buy your products or services you must create value during the sales conversation – before they commit to the investment required to have you create the value you promise once they become a client.

In other words – the sales conversation itself must create real value.

Simon explains that the following things don't create value in the sales conversation:

- Your company branding
- Your testimonials
- Your product specification or description
- Your promise of quality and service
- Your statement of purpose and why you exist
- Your expressions of values and culture

While they're important to have in place, none of these things create value for your prospect. They really just serve you!

Now I believe Simon deliberately used the term "create value" rather than "add value". He explains that if you want to give someone a reason to commit to you, ahead of all other alternatives, it's just not enough to be an "add on" – you must be the foundation… the base.

So, what DOES create value for your prospect in the sales conversation?

- You could help them to see possibility in their own situation that neither they, nor anyone else, has seen for them. Aspirational, yet achievable, transformation is a powerful form of value creation!
- You may demonstrate that you understand them and their circumstances at a deeper level than anyone else – that they are truly understood. Meeting someone who truly "gets them" is a powerful form of value creation!
- You might create such a powerful sense of risk reversal for them that they recognise you are the safest option for them to take. Safety is a powerful form of value creation!

- You could share a deeper and more profound insight into how their problem or need might be solved than anyone else, offering them a stronger set of options and alternatives than they knew were available to them. Optionality is a powerful form of value creation!

In short, if you want to persuade or influence someone to work with you or buy from you, then you must create more value than anyone else they meet in the sales conversation.

One way of adding value

As I said, your prospect has probably done a lot of homework and research before even seeing you.

The world is crowded with information and the issue today isn't about the quality of information, it's about the quantity of information – there is just too much of it and most likely your prospect has access to a number of comparably good options.

Research from Gartner's suggests that customers now spend at least 15% of their buying time just trying to "deconflict" competing information. It also shows that 55% of customers say they encounter an overwhelming amount of trustworthy information, while 44% struggle with the fact that seemingly trustworthy information, from different suppliers, was contradictory.

So your role as a persuader is to make your customer feel safer and more confident by helping them find the right questions to ask themselves, identify which information matters most and see consistent patterns in the information.

Simon Bowen explains it this way...

What doesn't work anymore is a salesperson that says *"I can get you more information on that"* or *"let me tell you what you need to know"*.

What is working is when the salesperson says *"there is a lot of information, let me help you to make sense of it"*.

As a smart persuader you'll guide prospects through the patterns of information, sharing evidence and prioritising simplification over detail.

Sense-making selling is much more likely to win high-quality, low-regret customers.

Another way of adding value

The COVID-19 crisis has reinforced what we already knew: to be an effective persuader it's more important than ever to understand your customer and it's critical that they realise that you "get them".

You see... we're all driven by different things. The EY Future Consumer Index researched 14,500 individuals in 20 countries and identified five different cohorts of consumers:

1. *Affordability first* (32% of consumers): Living within their means and budget, focusing less on brands and more on product functionality.
2. *Health first* (25%): Protecting their health and that of their family, choosing products they trust to be safe and minimising risks in the way that they shop.
3. *Planet first* (16%): Trying to minimise their impact on environment and buying brands that reflect their beliefs.
4. *Society first* (15%): Working together for the greater good, buying from organisations they find to be honest and transparent.
5. *Experience first* (12%): Living in the moment to make the most of life, often making them open to new products, brands, and experiences.

Obviously understanding your prospects persona will be critical in creating rapport.

Another change in the current environment

Currently we are living in "interesting times" with a lot of uncertainty regarding the future of our economy, and lots of talk about recession clouding our future.

Today you'll find that many of your clients and prospects want to feel safe and be understood. This is very different to only a few years ago when things were booming and clients were prepared to be bold and brave.

Here are three ways to positively influence prospects by showing it's safer to work with you or buy from you rather than anyone else:

1. Offer a *prescription* – tell them what they need to do step-by-step.
2. Remove risks and offer *protection*.
3. Offer a time-tested *proven strategy* to help you get ahead.

What's Next?

■ ■ ■

By now you'll realise that those who can influence and persuade others are going to get ahead of the pack. They will be able to improve their own circumstances, income and status by understanding that when you give other people what they want, you'll be able to get what you want.

Whether you're a parent persuading your children to live decent moral lives, a teacher inspiring student to rise to the top, or a businessman persuading clients to use your goods or services, you've now learned a better way to connect.

So thank you for reading this book — now it's up to you!

You've made the effort to purchase this book, you've taken the time to learn the knowledge to become a Power Negotiator. You've studied the skills of influential persuaders. Wouldn't it be a shame if you didn't put them into practice, because the power of the information in this book is not in the knowledge, but in its implementation?

See what I did? I used positive, positive, positive — negative.

Of course, the trouble with so many books is that when you've finished them, you're finished with what they have to tell you. What happens after that? Readers are often left to their own devices to try to take the next step and put the theory they have learned into action. This book is going to be a little bit different.

Now that we've covered a lot of ground in terms of theory the next step in your journey is going to involve putting this into practice and there are a number of ways that you can keep in touch with me and my thoughts.

I am are eager for the ideas in this book to work for you, so I have assembled a tool-kit of resources for you to help you become a Power Negotiator — just go to www.NegotiateInfulencePersuade. com. There you will be able to download a number of gifts and resources when you register your book.

I also suggest you subscribe to my daily newsletter at www. PropertyUpdate.com.au. This will help you keep up to date with our changing property markets as well as the latest information about money and success.

Then go to iTunes or your favourite podcast app or www. MichaelYardneyPodcast.com and subscribe to my weekly podcast — The Michael Yardney Podcast.

When you do, please email me and let me know about your success. I love getting emails from readers of my books who have successfully put my strategies to work.
Spend your time…wisely.

Michael Yardney
michael@metropole.com.au

About the Author

■ ■ ■

Michael Yardney has been voted one of Australia's 50 most influential Thought Leaders.

Michael is Australia's most trusted property commentator and his opinions are frequently quoted in the media and he has been featured in all major newspapers, finance and property magazines throughout Australia and in his regular segments on TV as well as on commercial radio.

And while he is best known as a property expert, Michael is also Australia's leading expert in the psychology of success and wealth creation.

Michael is a #1 best selling author of 9 books and frequently challenges traditional finance advice with innovative ideas on property investment, personal finance and wealth creation.

His wisdom stems from his personal experience and from mentoring over 2,500 business people, investors and entrepreneurs over the last decade and over the years Michael has probably educated more successful property investors than anyone else in Australia.

Michael is host of the popular Michael Yardney Podcast and writes regular columns for Yahoo Finance, Your Investment Property Magazine, and Your Mortgage.